Nick Vandome

Photoshop Elements 8

in easy steps

For Windows and Mac

In easy steps is an imprint of In Easy Steps Limited
Southfield Road · Southam
Warwickshire CV47 0FB · United Kingdom
www.ineasysteps.com

Notice of Liability
Every effort has been made to ensure that this book contains accurate
and current information. However, In Easy Steps Limited and the
author shall not be liable for any loss or damage suffered by readers
as a result of any information contained herein.

Trademarks
Photoshop® is a registered trademark of Adobe Systems Incorporated.
All other trademarks are acknowledged as belonging to their
respective companies.

In Easy Steps Limited supports The Forest Stewardship Council (FSC),
the leading international forest certification organisation. All our titles
that are printed on Greenpeace approved FSC certified paper carry the
FSC logo.

Mixed Sources
Product group from well-managed
forests and other controlled sources
www.fsc.org Cert no. SGS-COC-005998
© 1996 Forest Stewardship Council

Printed and bound in the United Kingdom

ISBN 978-1-84078-392-6

Contents

3 First Digital Steps 55

4 Quick Wins 71

5 Beyond the Basics 95

1 Introducing Elements

Photoshop Elements is a digital image editing program that comprehensively spans the gap between very basic programs and professional-level ones. This chapter introduces the various sections and modes of Elements and shows how access them. It also shows how to quickly get up and running with this powerful, flexible and creative image editing program.

About Elements

Photoshop Elements is the offspring of the professional-level image editing program, Photoshop. Photoshop is somewhat unusual in the world of computer software, in that it is widely accepted as being the best program of its type on the market. If professional designers or photographers are using an image editing program, it will almost certainly be Photoshop. However, two of the potential drawbacks to Photoshop are the cost (approximately $600) and its complexity. This is where Elements comes into its own. Adobe (the makers of Photoshop and Elements) have recognized that the majority of digital imaging users (i.e. the consumer market) want something with the basic power of Photoshop, but with enough user-friendly features to make it easy to use. With the explosion in the digital camera market, a product was needed to meet the needs of a new generation of image editors – and that product is Elements.

Elements contains the same powerful editing/color management tools as the full version of Photoshop and it also includes a number of versatile features for sharing images and for creating artistic projects, such as slide shows, cards, calendars and online photo albums for the Web. It also has valuable help features, such as the Guided Edit mode, which explains what different items can be used for and gives a step-by-step guide to various digital editing techniques:

Don't forget

Photoshop Elements can be bought online from computer and software sites, or at computer software stores. There are Windows and Mac versions of the program.

Special effects

One of the great things about using Elements with digital images is that it provides numerous fun and creative options for turning mediocre images into eye-catching works of art. This is achieved through a wide variety of artwork and effects:

Advanced features

In addition to user-friendly features, Elements also has more advanced functions, such as the histogram:

Don't forget

The histogram displays the tonal range of the colors in an image.

9

Welcome Screen

When you first open Elements, you will be presented with the Welcome Screen. This offers initial advice about working with Elements and also provides options for creating new files, or opening existing ones. The Welcome Screen appears by default but this can be altered once you become more familiar with Elements.

Welcome Screen functions

The Mac version of Elements has a similar, but not identical, Welcome Screen.

10

1 Options for organizing photos, editing them and using them in a variety of creative ways

2 Click on the Learn More buttons to find out about certain functions in Elements

3 Click on the Organize button to go to that area

The Welcome Screen can be accessed at any time by selecting Window> Welcome from the Editor Menu bar.

4 Click on the Edit button to go to that area

Editor Mode

From the Welcome Screen the Elements Editor interface can be accessed. This is a combination of the work area (where images are opened and edited), menus, toolbars, a toolbox and panels. At first it can seem a little daunting, but Elements has been designed to offer as much help as possible as you proceed through the digital editing process.

The components of the Elements Editor are:

Menu bar   Options bar   Shortcuts bar   Panels bin

Toolbox   Project Bin   Work area   Open panels

Don't forget

Editor mode has a Full Edit function, a Quick Edit option and a Guided Edit mode. Full Edit is used for general, and advanced, image editing. Quick Edit can be used for automated editing in one step, and Guided mode offers step-by-step guidance and advice.

Project Bin

The Project Bin is a feature that can be accessed from the Editor in either Full Edit or Quick Edit mode. The Project Bin enables you to quickly access all of the images that you have open within the Editor. To use the Project Bin:

1 Open two or more images. The most recently opened one will be the one that is active in the Editor

2 All open images are shown here in the Project Bin

3 Double-click on an image in the Project Bin to make that the active one for editing

Quick Edit Mode

Quick Edit mode contains a number of functions that can be selected from a panel and applied to an image, without the need to manually apply all of the commands. To do this:

1 In the Editor, click on the Edit Quick button

2 The currently active image is displayed within the Quick Edit window

Don't forget

For an in-depth look at Quick Edit mode, have a look at Chapter Four.

3 Select one of the commands to have it applied to the active image. This can either be applied by clicking on the Auto button or by dragging the appropriate slider to apply the command

Guided Edit Mode

Guided Edit mode is similar to Quick Fix mode, except that it focuses on common tasks for editing digital images and shows you how to perform them. To use Guided Edit mode:

1 In Edit mode, click on the Edit Guided button

2 The currently active image is displayed within the Guided Edit window

Don't forget

Guided Edit mode is a great place to start if you are new to image editing, or feel unsure about anything to do with it.

3 Select one of the actions that you want to perform. This will take you to a step-by-step process for undertaking the required action

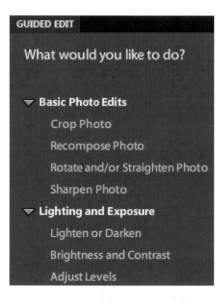

Organizer Mode

The Organizer mode contains a number of functions for sorting, viewing and finding multiple images. To use the Organizer:

1 In Editor mode, click on the Organizer button

2 The Media Browser displays thumbnails of your photos, and also has functions for sorting and finding images

Don't forget

Images displayed in the Media Browser can be located anywhere on your computer. The thumbnails in Media Browser are just references to the originals, wherever they are stored.

3 In the Media Browser, click on the Date View button

↩ Undo	↪ Redo	🖥 Display ▾
✓ Thumbnail View		Ctrl+Alt+1
Import Batch		Ctrl+Alt+2
Folder Location		Ctrl+Alt+3
Date View		Ctrl+Alt+D

4 This displays a calendar interface that can be used to view images that were captured on a specific date. Click here to move through the calendar

Don't forget

The Mac version of Elements does not have an Organizer mode. Instead, this function is undertaken by the Adobe Bridge program. For more information about this see pages 24–29.

Create Mode

Create mode is where you can release your artistic flair and start designing photo books and photo collages. It can also be used to create slide shows and to put your images onto disc, using the VCD format. To use Create mode:

1 In either the Editor or the Organizer, click on the Create button

2 Select one of the Create projects. Each project has a wizard that takes you through the create process

Don't forget

For an in-depth look at Create mode have a look at Chapter Ten.

16

3 Create mode can be used to create a variety of artistic projects, containing your own images

Share Mode

Share mode can be used to distribute your images to family and friends in a variety of creative ways. To use Share mode:

1 In either the Editor or the Organizer, click on the Share button

2 Select one of the Share options

Don't forget

For an in-depth look at Share mode have a look at Chapter Ten.

3 The projects have templates and wizards that takes you through the process of creating the project for sharing

Menu Bar

In the Editor, the Menu bar contains menus that provide all of the functionality for the workings of Elements. Some of these functions can also be achieved through the use of the other components of Elements, such as the Toolbox, the Shortcuts bar, the Options bar and the panels. However, the Menu bar is where all of the commands needed for the digital editing process can be accessed in one place.

Menu bar menus

Don't forget

The Mac version of Elements also has a Photoshop Elements menu on the Menu bar. This contains the Preferences options.

18

Beware

Elements does not support the CMYK color model for editing digital images. This could be an issue if you use a commercial printer.

- File. This has standard commands for opening, saving and printing images, and also commands for creating panoramas (Photomerge) and accessing online services from Adobe

- Edit. This contains commands for undoing previous operations, and standard copy and paste techniques

- Image. This contains commands for altering the size, shape and position of an image. It also contains more advanced functions, such as changing the color mode of an image

- Enhance. This contains commands for editing the color elements of an image. It also contains quick-fix options

- Layer. This contains commands for working with different layers within an image

- Select. This contains commands for working with areas that have been selected within an image, with one of the selection tools in the Toolbox

- Filter. This contains numerous filters that can be used to apply special effects to an image

- View. This contains commands for changing the size at which an image is displayed, and also options for showing or hiding rulers and grid lines

- Window. This contains commands for changing the way multiple images are displayed, and also options for displaying all of the components of Elements

- Help. This contains the various Help options

Toolbox

The Toolbox contains tools for adding items to an image (such as shapes and text), selecting areas of an image and also for applying editing techniques. Some of the tools have more than one option, in which case, they have a small black triangle at the bottom right of the default tool. To access additional tools in the Toolbox:

Click and hold here to access additional tools for a particular item

Working with the Toolbox

By default, the Toolbox is docked at the left of the main Editor window. However, it can be removed and dragged anywhere within the main window. To do this:

1 Click on the two arrows to view the Toolbox in one column. Click on the cross to close it

2 Click and drag here to move the Toolbox around the Editor window. Drag it back to its original location to redock it at the left of the window

Don't forget

The tools that have additional options are: the Marquee tools, the Lasso tools, the Magic Selection Brush tool, the Healing Brush tools, the Type tools, the Crop tools, the Eraser tools, the Brush tools, the Stamp tools, the Object tools (e.g. the Rectangle tool), the Blur tool and the Sponge tool.

Don't forget

For full details of the Toolbox functions, see the inside front cover of the book.

Hot tip

If the Toolbox is not visible, select Window> Tools from the Menu bar.

Options Bar

The Options bar provides attributes that can be set for a selected tool from the Toolbox. For instance, if the Eraser tool is selected, the Options bar offers choices for the type of eraser that can be used, its size, its mode and its opacity level. For each tool, a different set of options is available.

Using the Options bar

1 Click on a tool in the Toolbox (in this example it is the Magic Wand tool)

2 Select the options for the tool in the Options bar

| | Tolerance: 32 | ✔ Anti-alias | ✔ Contiguous | All Layers |

3 Apply the tool to an image. The tool will maintain the settings in the Options bar until they are changed

Panels

Elements uses panels to group together similar editing functions and provide quick access to certain techniques. The available panels are:

- Adjustments. This can be used to add or make editing changes to adjustment layers in the Layers panel

- Color Swatches. This is a panel for selecting colors that can then be applied to parts of an image or elements that have been added to it

- Content. This contains graphical elements that can be added to images. This includes backgrounds, frame shapes and artistic text

- Effects. This contains special effects and styles that can be applied to an entire image or a selected part of an image. There are also filters which have their own dialog boxes in which settings can be applied and adjusted. Layer Styles can also be applied to elements within an image

- Favorites. This is where favorite graphical elements from the Content panel can be store and retrieved quickly

- Histogram. This displays a graph of the tonal range of the colors in an image. It is useful for assessing the overall exposure of an image and it changes as an image is edited

- Info. This displays information about an image, or a selected element within it. This includes details about the color in an image or the position of a certain item

- Layers. This enables several layers to be included within an image. This can be useful if you want to add elements to an existing image, such as shapes or text. Layers can also be used to merge two separate images together

- Navigator. This can be used to move around an image and magnify certain areas of it

- Undo History. This can be used to undo all, or some, of the editing steps that have been performed. Every action is displayed in the Undo History panel and these actions can be reversed by dragging the slider at the side of the panel upwards

Don't forget

For more information about working with layers and adjustment layers, see Chapter Seven, pages 129–130.

Hot tip

The panels are located in the Panel Bin, which is at the right of the Editor window. This can be collapsed or expanded by selecting Window>Panel Bin from the Menu bar.

21

...cont'd

Working with panels

By default, all panels are minimized and grouped in the Panel Bin. However, it is possible to open one or more panel so that they are displayed independently from the Panel Bin. To work with panels:

 Panels are grouped together in the Panel Bin at the right of the work area

 Click and drag here to move a panel away from the bin (or move a detached panel back into the bin)

 Click here on the on the top bar to expand or contract a panel

 Every panel has its own menu; its options depend on the functions within the panel

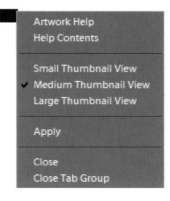

Preferences

A number of preferences can be set within Elements to determine the way the program operates. It is perfectly acceptable to leave all of the default settings as they are, but as you become more familiar with the program you may want to change some of the preference settings. Preferences can be accessed by selecting Edit>Preferences from the Menu bar, and the available ones are:

- General. This contains a variety of options for selecting items, such as shortcut keys

- Saving Files. This determines the way Elements saves files

- Performance. This determines how Elements allocates memory when processing editing tasks. It also determines how Elements allocates disk space when processing editing tasks (scratch disks). If you require more memory for editing images (image editing can be a very memory-intensive process) you can do this by allocating up to four scratch disks on your hard drive. These act as extra areas from which memory can be used during the editing process

- Display & Cursors. This determines how cursors operate when certain tools are selected

- Transparency. This determines the color, or transparency, of the background on which an open image resides

- Units & Rulers. This determines the unit of measurement used by items, such as rulers

- Guides and Grids. This determines the color and format of any guides and grids that are used

- Plug-Ins. This displays any plug-ins that have been downloaded to enhance image editing with Elements

- Type. This determines the way text appears when it is added to images

- Organize & Share. These preferences open in the Organizer mode and offer a collection of preferences that are applicable to these functions. These are General, Files, Folder Location View, Editing, Camera or Card Reader, Scanner, Date View, Keyword Tags and Albums, Sharing, Adobe Partner Services and Auto-Analyzer Options

Don't forget

Each preference has its own dialog box in which the specific preference settings can be made.

Don't forget

Guides and grids can be accessed from the View menu in Editor mode.

Hot tip

The Organize & Share preferences can be accessed by selecting Edit>Preferences from the Menu bar in either the Editor or the Organizer. This option is not available with the Mac version of Elements.

Elements for the Mac

For previous versions of Elements, some have included a Mac version while others have not. However, Elements 8 comes in versions for both Windows and Mac.

The main editing functions for the Mac version are very similar to those for the Windows version. These are:

- Full Edit

- Quick Edit

- Guided Edit

The Welcome window enables you to open new documents, import images from a camera or a scanner, or organize images with the accompanying Bridge program.

Don't forget

Adobe Bridge is a program that comes with Elements for the Mac, that is used for organizing, tagging and searching for images.

The editing interface is also very similar in the Mac version.

New features

In Elements 8 there are a number of new features that have not been included with previous Mac versions of Elements. These can be used in the same way as those described in this book. These features include:

- Recomposing without distortion (see Chapter Three, page 60)

- Touch-up Quick Edits (see Chapter Four, page 80)

- Scene Cleaner (see Chapter Four, page 82)

- Merging Exposures (see Chapter Four, page 84)

The Mac version of Elements also has five buttons that are not available in the Windows version. These are located at the top of the Editor window.

Open New File   Save   Arrange Open Files

Adobe Bridge   Help options

Beware

The Mac version of Elements does not have the functions that can be accessed from the Organizer in the Windows version.

Differences

The main differences between the Windows and Mac versions of Elements are in the way images and media are organized and tagged. In the Windows version this is done within Elements with the Organizer area. However, the Mac version uses a separate program, Adobe Bridge, for organizing media and this is packaged with the Mac version of the program. This can be accessed from the Bridge button at the top of the Elements main window.

Elements can also be used as an image editor if you are using the Mac iPhoto program for organizing your photos. To do this, you can set Elements as your editor within the iPhoto Preferences: select iPhoto on the Menu bar, then select Preferences. In the Preferences window, click on the General tab and select the Edit Photo option. Select the In Application option and browse the Applications folder and select Elements.

Don't forget

iPhoto is an image organizing program that comes pre-installed with new Macs. It can also be used for some editing functions, but it is not as powerful or as flexible as Elements for editing.

...cont'd

Using Bridge

The main purposes of using Bridge are to view all your images and also tag them so that you can search for specific images or subjects. To access Bridge:

1 Click on this button in the Elements Editor

2 The default view of Bridge is the Essentials area, where you can view your folder structure and images

Hot tip

Items can be added to the Favorites tab by dragging folders from the main window.

3 Click on the Favorites tab to view areas on your Mac to which you want to have quick access

4 Click on the Folders tab to view your standard navigation structure. Browse the folders and select one to view its contents

5 Once a folder has been selected, the images are displayed in the main window

Don't forget

The file path of the selected folder is shown at the top of the Bridge window. This shows the location of the images that are displayed in the Content area.

6 Click here to view the main window items as (from left to right), Thumbnails, Details and List

7 At the bottom of the Bridge window, drag this slider to change the size at which images are displayed

Working with metadata

Metadata is information that can be attached to digital images to help with searching and identification. Some metadata is generated when digital images are captured and other items, such as keywords, can be added within Bridge. The Metadata tab is visible within the different areas of Bridge and contains camera information about a selected image.

...cont'd

Metadata can also be added to specific images. To do this:

1 Click on an image in the main Essentials window. This will be displayed in the Preview window within Bridge

2 Click on the Keywords tab to view the available keywords

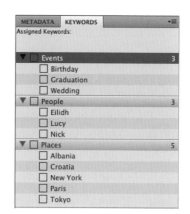

3 Click here to (from left to right) add a keyword sub-category, a keyword category or delete a selected item

4 Check on the box next to a keyword to have that keyword applied to the selected image

Searching for items

One of the main uses for metadata and keywords is to search for images containing certain details. To do this:

1 Click on the Filter tab to access categories of metadata. Click on an arrow to view the sub-categories for each item

2 Under Keywords, click on a keyword to see all of the items that have had that keyword attached to them

Filmstrip

Click on the Filmstrip tab to view thumbnails of images

Metadata

Click on the Metadata tab to view details of images, such as Date Created, Size, Type and Dimensions.

Hot tip

In the Metadata window, ratings can be added to specific images. To do this, click on the rating area and click on the number of stars that you want to apply to the image. Images can then be searched for using different ratings.

Getting Help

One of the differences between Elements and the full version of Photoshop is the amount of assistance and guidance offered by each program. Since Photoshop is aimed more at the professional end of the market, the level of help is confined largely to the standard help directory that serves as an online manual. Elements also contains this, but in addition it has the Getting Started option which is designed to take users through the digital image editing process as smoothly as possible. The Getting Started option offers general guidance about digital imaging techniques and there are also help items that can be accessed by selecting Help from the Menu bar. These include online help, information on available plug-ins for Elements, tutorials and support details.

Using the help files

Don't forget

For the Mac version of Elements the Help function can also be accessed from the Help button at the top of the Editor window.

1 Select Photoshop Elements Help from the Help menu and click Contents or Index. Then click once on an item to display it in the main window

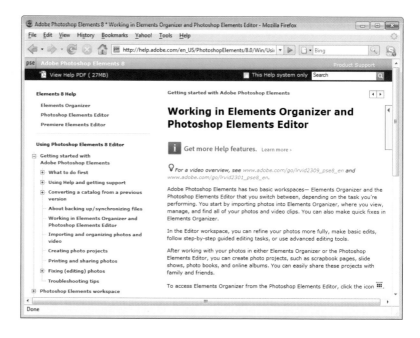

2 Organizing Images

This chapter shows how to download digital images via Elements and then how to view and organize them. It also shows how you can tag images, so that they are easy to find, and it details how to look for images according to the date on which they were taken, or the location on a map at which they were originally captured. It also covers how to expand your digital options by using video.

Obtaining Images

One of the first tasks in Elements is to download images so that you can start editing and sharing them. This can be done from a variety of devices, but the process is similar for all of them. To download images into Elements:

Don't forget

For a lot of digital cameras, the Photo Downloader window will appear automatically once the camera is connected to the computer. However, if this does not happen it will have to be accessed manually as shown here.

1 Access the Organizer by clicking on this button in the Editor

2 Select File>Get Photos and Videos from the Menu bar and select the type of device from which you want to load images into Elements

From Camera or Card Reader...	Ctrl+G
From Scanner...	Ctrl+U
From Files and Folders...	Ctrl+Shift+G
By Searching...	

Hot tip

Images can also be downloaded from existing files and folders on a computer. This means that they will be added to the Organizer's database and you will be able to apply all of its features to the images.

3 If you select From Camera and Card Reader, click under Get Photos From to select a specific device

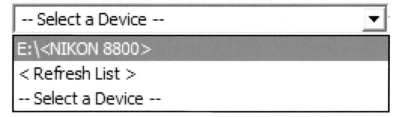

Get Photos from:

-- Select a Device --

E:\<NIKON 8800>

< Refresh List >

-- Select a Device --

Don't forget

The Mac version of Elements uses the Adobe Photo Downloader for obtaining images, which are downloaded into the Bridge organizing program. The Downloader is accessed from the File menu on the Editor Menu bar.

4 The images to be downloaded are displayed here, next to the device from which they will be downloaded

5 Click here to select a destination for the selected images and click the Get Photos button to download them

6 As the images are being downloaded, the following window is displayed

7 After the files have been copied they are then imported into Elements

8 Click on the OK button so that the images are imported. They can then be viewed in the Organizer and opened in the Editor

Hot tip

Images can also be downloaded from a pen drive. To do this, insert the pen drive and use the From Camera or Card Reader download option. You will then be able to download the images in the same way as with a camera or card reader.

33

Media Browser

The Media Browser is the function within the Organizer that is used to view, find and sort images. When using the Media Browser, images have to be actively added to it so it can then catalog them. Once images have been downloaded, the Media Browser acts as a window for viewing and sorting your images, no matter where they are located. Aspects of the Media Browser include the following:

34

1 Drag this slider to view images at different sizes in the Media Browser

2 Main window for viewing images

3 Options for adding tags to images and creating albums of similar images

4 Click here to select options for how images are displayed

Magnification slider for changing the size at which images are viewed in the main window:

Accessing images

To access images within the Media Browser:

1 Click on images to select them individually, or as a group

2 Drag here to scroll through images within the main window

3 Double-click on an image to view it in the whole Media Browser window

Full Screen Preview

From within the Media Browser it is possible to view all of your images, or a selection of them, at full screen size. In addition, music can be added to create an impressive slide show effect. To use the Full Screen Preview:

1 In the Media Browser, click here and select View, Edit, Organize in Full Screen, or press F11

2 The image is displayed, with the Quick Edit and Quick Organize panels displayed at the side of the window

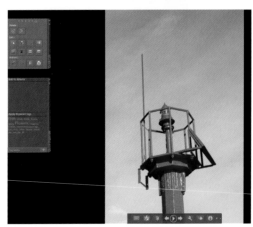

Hot tip

Press Esc to return to the Media Browser from either Full Screen Preview or Full Screen Compare.

3 Use these buttons to (from left to right) show or hide the filmstrip of images, show or hide the Quick Edit panel and show or hide the Quick Organize panel

4 Use these buttons to (from left to right) move to the previous image, play all images as a slide show and move to the next image

5 Use these buttons to (from left to right) view options for playing a slide show, select transitions for a slide show and view the general properties of an image

Full Screen Compare

In addition to viewing individual images at full screen size, it is also possible to compare two images next to each other. This can be a very useful way of checking the detail of similar images, particularly for items such as focus and lighting. To compare images using Full Screen Compare:

1 In Full Screen Preview, click here on the toolbar and select an option for comparing images

2 Click on two images in the image pane

3 Click on this button on the toolbar. This enables zooming on both images simultaneously

4 Drag on this slider, or click the zoom icon

5 The images are displayed and the zoom command is applied to both of them

Don't forget

Only two images can be compared at the same time in Full Screen Compare. If you select a third image while in Full Screen Compare, this will replace one of the other two images.

Hot tip

Full Screen Compare is a good way to compare two similar images, as far as their image quality is concerned.

Auto-Analyzer

Once photos have been downloaded into the Organizer it is possible to run a function that analyzes several elements relating to the quality of the images. Once this has been done the elements are added as tags to the images. This creates a quick visual guide to the quality of photos, which can be viewed in the Organizer. To use the Auto-Analyzer:

Beware

If you do not make a selection, the Auto-Analyzer will run over all of your photos. Depending on the number of photos, this can take a considerable amount of time.

1 In the Organizer, select the photos which you want to be analyzed. (If you do not select any images, the Auto-Analyzer will be performed over the whole collection)

2 Select Edit>Run Auto-Analyzer from the Menu bar. This will then be performed over the selected images (or the whole collection)

3 The Auto-Analyzer tags are added to the images

4 Double-click on an image

High Quality, Long Shot, Small Group, In Focus, Too Dark

5 The tags that have been added are shown underneath the image. These are all elements that have been identified by the Auto-Analyzer

High Quality, Long Shot, Small Group, In Focus, Too Dark

6 The tags are automatically added to the Keywords Tag panel in the Organizer. Check on the box next to a tag to view all of the images with a specific tag

Stacks

Since digital cameras make it quick, easy and cheap to capture dozens, or hundreds, of images on a single memory card it is no surprise that most people are now capturing more images than ever before. One result of this is that it is increasingly tempting to take several shots of the same subject, just to try and capture the perfect image. The one drawback with this is that when it comes to organizing your images on a computer it can become time-consuming to work your way through all of your near-identical shots. The Media Browser offers a useful solution to this by enabling the stacking of similar images, so that you can view a single thumbnail rather than several. To do this:

Beware

You can remove images from a stack by selecting the stack in the Media Browser and selecting Edit>Stack>Flatten Stack from the Menu bar. However, this will remove all of the images, apart from the top one, from the Media Browser. This does not remove them from your hard drive, although there is an option to do this too, if you wish.

40

1. Select the images that you want to stack in the Media Browser

2. Select Edit>Stack>Stack Selected Photos from the Menu bar

3. The images are stacked into a single thumbnail and the existence of the stack is indicated by this icon

4. To view all of the stacked images, click here

5. Click here to return to all of the photos in the Media Browser

Don't forget

To revert stacked images to their original state, select Edit>Stack>Unstack Photos from the Menu bar.

Version Sets

When working with digital images it is commonplace to create several different versions from a single image. This could be to use one for printing and one for use on the Web, or because there are elements of an image that you want to edit. Instead of losing track of images that have been edited it is possible to create stacked thumbnails of edited images, which are known as version sets. These can include the original image and all of the edited versions. Version sets can be created and added to from either the Media Browser or the Editor. To do this:

1 Open an image

2 Make editing changes to the image in either Full Edit or Quick Fix mode

3 Select File>Save As from the Menu bar

4 Check on the Save in Version Set with Original box and click Save

5 A dialog box alerts you to the fact that the image has been edited but the original has not been altered. Click OK

6 The original image and the edited one are grouped together in a stack, and the fact that it is a version set is denoted by this icon

7 To view all of the images in a version set, select the set and select Edit>Version Set>Reveal Photos in Version Set from the Menu bar

Don't forget

The other version set menu options are Flatten Version Set, and Revert to Original. The latter deletes all of the other versions except the original image.

41

Tagging Images

As your digital image collection begins to grow on your computer it is increasingly important to be able to keep track of your images and find the ones you want, when you want them. One way of doing this is by assigning specific tags to images. You can then search for images according to the tags that have been added to them. The tagging function is accessed from the Task Pane within the Organizer. To add tags to images:

Don't forget

The Task Pane can also be accessed by selecting Window>Show Task Pane from the Organizer Menu bar.

Hot tip

When you create a new category you can also choose a new icon too.

① If the Task Pane is not visible, select Window>Show Task Pane from the Menu Bar, or click here on the right border of the Media Browser to expand the Task Pane

② Click here to access the currently available tags

③ Click here to access sub-categories for a particular category

④ Click here to add categories, or sub-categories, of your own choice

42

5 Enter a name for the new category, or sub-category, and click on the OK button

Create Sub-Category

Sub-Category Name

Croatia

Parent Category or Sub-Category

Places

OK   Cancel

Hot tip

Multiple tags can be added to the same image. This gives you greater flexibility when searching for images.

6 Select the required images in the Media Browser

7 Drag a tag onto one of the selected images

Don't forget

Tagged images can still be searched for by using a sub-category tag, even though they are denoted in the Media Browser by the tag for the main category.

8 The images are tagged with the icon that denotes the main category, rather than the sub-category

People Recognition

People shots are popular in most types of photography. However, this can result in hundreds, or thousands, of photos of different people. In Elements there is a feature that enables you to tag people throughout your collections. This is known as people recognition. To use this:

1 In the Organizer, either select individual images, or do not select any to have people recognition applied to the whole collection

2 Select Find>Find People for Tagging from the Menu bar

3 The Organizer will analyze each photo and display a prompt box for each new face

4 Enter a name in the prompt box

5 When the next face is identified the prompt box will ask if this is the same as other faces that have already been recognized. Click on the green tick if this is the correct face

Is this Nick?

6 The tag for each name entered will automatically be added to the keyword tags

Nick

People Recognition really comes into its own when you have tagged dozens, or hundreds, of photos. You can then view all of the photos containing a specific person.

7 Check on the box next to a name to display the binoculars. All of the tagged images are displayed within the Organizer

3/3/2010   3/3/2010

45

Searching for Images

Once images have been tagged they can be searched for using both of these options. To do this:

46

1 For tags and collections, click on this box so that the binoculars are showing

2 Drag one of the icons below the timeline in the Media Browser

3 All matching items for a search are shown together within the Media Browser

4 Click on the Show All button to return to the rest of the images

Albums

Albums in Elements are similar to physical photo albums: they are a location into which you can store all your favorite groups of images. Once they have been stored there they can easily be found when required. To create albums:

1 In the Organizer, click on the Albums tab and select New Album

2 Enter a name for the new album and click Done

3 Select the images that you would like included in the new album

4 Drag the selected images into the new album

5 Click here to view all of the images in a specific album

Smart Albums

A further development of the Albums idea is that of Smart Albums. These are albums to which certain criteria are attached. Any subsequently downloaded images that contain the criteria are automatically added to the relevant Smart Album. To do this:

1 In the Organizer, click on the Albums tab and select New Smart Album

2 Set the criteria for the Smart Album. This can include the filename containing a certain word or other similar attributes for the image

3 Click on the OK button

4 All of the images that match the criteria in the Smart Album are displayed

Hot tip

You can include several different search criteria for each Smart Album. For instance, you might have one criteria where the filename has to include Paris and another where the camera model is Nikon.

5 Click here to display all of the images in a Smart Album

6 Any new images with this criteria will automatically be included in the Smart Album

49

Date View

Date View is a function that offers the facility for viewing downloaded images in a calendar format. This can be viewed for either a year, a month or a day. The images are placed in the calendar according to the date on which they were taken, edited or downloaded. To use Date View:

1 In the Organizer, click here and select Date View

2 Click here to move through the calendar

3 Double-click on an image to view all of the items for that specific day in the full window

4 Select a day and click here to view all of the images for that day in a slide show

5 Select an option here to view the calendar in Year, Month or Day format

Map View

Map View is a function that enables you to place an image on a map, according to where it was taken. To do this:

1 In the Media Browser, select the required images and select Edit>Place on Map from the Menu bar

2 Enter a location and click on the Find button

3 The location will be searched for and displayed in the Look Up Address window. Click on the OK button if this is the correct location

4 Once images have been added to the map, this is denoted by a red circle

5 Click on a red circle to display the images for that location

Opening and Saving Images

Once you have captured images with a digital camera, or a scanner, and stored them on your computer, you can open them in Elements. There are a number of options for this:

Open command

1 Select File>Open from the Menu bar

2 Select an image from your hard drive and click Open

Open As command

This can be used to open a file in a different file format from its original format. To do this:

1 Select File>Open As from the Menu bar

2 Select an image and select the file format. Click Open

Saving images

When saving digital images, it is always a good idea to save them in at least two different file formats, particularly if layered objects, such as text and shapes, have been added. One of these formats should be the proprietary Photoshop format PSD or PDD. The reason for using this is that it will retain all of the layered information within an image. So, if a text layer has been added, this will still be available for editing at a future date, once it has been saved and closed.

The other format, that an image should be saved in, is the one most appropriate for the use to which it is going to be put. Therefore, images that are going to be used on the Web should be saved as JPEG, GIF or PNG files, while an image that is going to be used for printing should be saved in another format, such as TIFF. Once images have been saved in these formats, all of the layered information within them becomes flattened into a single layer and it will not be possible to edit this once the image has been saved. By default, images are saved in the same format as the one in which they were opened.

Working with Video

As well as using Elements for viewing and organizing photos, it can also be used in the same way with video. Video can be imported into Elements in a number of ways:

- From a camera that has video recording capabilities

- From a digital video camera

- From a cell/mobile phone

- From video that has been created in the Elements Premiere program. This is a companion program to Elements and is used to manipulate and edit video. It can be bought in a package with Elements, or individually. See www.adobe.com/products/premiereel/ for more details

To download video into Elements:

1 Connect the device containing the video. Select the required device and download in the same way as for photos

2 The video is downloaded and displayed in the Organizer in the same way as photos

3 Video clips are identified by this symbol

Don't forget

Elements Premiere can be bought as a package with Elements, or it can be bought individually. At the time of writing there is only a Windows version of Premiere Elements available.

53

Beware

Video files are usually a lot larger in size than photos, and if you have a lot of them they will take up a lot of space on your computer.

...cont'd

Viewing video

To view video clips:

1 Double-click on the clip in the Organizer. The Elements video player will open and play the video clip

2 Use the controls underneath the video window to navigate through the clip and adjust the volume

Don't forget

The Find>By Media Type option can also be used to find audio files, projects and PDFs.

Finding video

To find video clips within Elements:

1 In the Organizer, select Find>By Media Type>Video from the Menu bar

3 First Digital Steps

This chapter shows how to get up and running with digital image editing, and details some effective editing techniques for improving digital images, such as improving the overall color, removing unwanted items and changing the size and shape of images.

Color Enhancements

Some of the simplest, but most effective editing changes, that can be made to digital images are color enhancements. These can help to transform a mundane image into a stunning one, and Elements offers a variety of methods for achieving this. Some of these are verging towards the professional end of image editing, while others are done almost automatically by Elements. These are known as Auto adjustments and some simple manual adjustments can also be made to the brightness and contrast of an image. All of these color enhancement features can be accessed from the Enhance menu on the Menu bar.

Auto Levels

This automatically adjusts the overall color tone in an image in relation to the lightest and darkest points in the image:

Auto Contrast

This automatically adjusts the contrast in an image:

Hot tip

Another Auto command on the Enhance menu is Auto Smart Fix. This can be used to automatically edit all of the color balance of an image in one step. However, the results can sometimes be less than perfect, so it is important to review the changes carefully to make sure they are better than the original.

Hot tip

Two other options for color enhancement are the Burn tool and the Dodge tool in the Toolbox. The Burn tool can be dragged over areas in an image to make them darker and the Dodge tool can be dragged over areas to make them lighter.

Auto Color Correction

This automatically adjusts all the color elements within an image:

Adjust Brightness/Contrast

This can be used to manually adjust the brightness and contrast in an image:

1 Select Enhance>Adjust Lighting>Brightness/Contrast from the Menu bar

2 Drag the sliders to adjust the image brightness and contrast

3 Click on the OK button

Don't forget

Apply small amounts of Brightness and Contrast at a time when you are editing an image. This will help ensure that the end result does not look too unnatural.

Hot tip

Always make sure that the Preview box is checked when you are applying color enhancements. This will display the changes as you make them and before they are applied to the image.

57

...cont'd

Adjust Shadows/Highlights

One problem that most photographers encounter at some point, is where part of an image is exposed correctly while another part is either over- or under-exposed. If this is corrected using general color correction techniques, such as levels or brightness and contrast, the poorly exposed area may be improved, but at the expense of the area that was correctly exposed initially. To overcome this, the Shadows/Highlights command can be used to adjust particular tonal areas of an image. To do this:

58

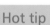

Hot tip

Adjusting shadows can make a significant improvement to an image in which one area is underexposed and the rest is correctly exposed.

 1 Open an image where one part is correctly exposed and another part is incorrectly exposed

2 Select Enhance> Adjust Lighting> Shadows/Highlights from the Menu bar

3 Make the required adjustments using the sliders or by entering figures in the boxes

Shadows/Highlights		
Learn more about: Shadows/Highlights	OK	
	Cancel	
Lighten Shadows:	50 %	✓ Preview
Darken Highlights:	0 %	
Midtone Contrast:	0 %	

4 Click OK

5 The poorly exposed areas of the image have been corrected, without altering the rest of the properly exposed image

Cropping

Cropping is a technique that can be used to remove unwanted areas of an image and highlight the main subject. The area to be cropped can only be selected as a rectangle. To crop an image:

1 Select the Crop tool from the Toolbox

2 Click and drag on an image to select the area to be cropped. The area that is selected is retained and the area to be cropped appears grayed-out

Hot tip

The Options bar for the Crop tool has an option for selecting preset sizes for the crop tool. This results in the crop being in specific proportions. For instance, if you want to print an image at 10 x 8 size, you can use this preset crop size to ensure that the cropped image is at the correct proportions. The image dialog box will also be updated accordingly.

3 Click and drag on these markers to resize the crop area

4 Click on the check mark to accept the changes, or the circle to reject them

Resizing without Distortion

Instead of cropping an image there may be times when you want to resize an image but keep the background as intact as possible. This can be done with the Recompose tool. To use this:

1 In the Editor, open the image that you want to recompose

60

2 Select the Recompose tool from the Toolbox (this is grouped with the Crop tool)

3 Click on the image and drag on the resizing handles. At this point, the whole image will be resized, creating distortion to foreground subjects

4 On the Options bar, click on the Mark for Protection button

5 Draw roughly over the area that you want to protect

As well as protecting elements in an image, items can also be marked for removal. This means that when the image is resized anything that has been marked in this way will disappear. To do this, click on the Mark for Removal button and draw on the required element in the same way as for protecting an item in Step 5.

6 Recompose the image in the same way as in Step 3. The foreground subject remains undistorted while the background is resized

7 To restrict the proportion of the resized image, select one of the Preset options on the Options bar

Preset: No Restriction ▼

No Restriction
Use Photo Ratio
2.5 x 2 in
3 x 5 in
4 x 6 in
5 x 5 in
5 x 7 in
8 x 10 in

61

Cloning

Cloning is a technique that can be used to copy one area of an image over another. This can be used to cover up small imperfections in an image, such as a dust mark or a spot, and also to copy or remove large items in an image, such as a person.

To clone items:

1 Select the Clone Stamp tool from the Toolbox

2 Set the Clone Stamp options in the Options bar

3 Hold down Alt and click on the image to select a source point from which the cloning will start

4 Drag the cursor to copy everything over which the selection point marker passes

Pattern Cloning

The Pattern Stamp tool can be used to copy a selected pattern over an image, or a selected area of an image. To do this:

1 Select the Pattern Stamp tool from the Toolbox

2 Click here in the Options bar to select a pattern

3 Click and drag on an image to copy the selected pattern over it

Don't forget

The Pattern Stamp tool is grouped in the Toolbox with the Clone Stamp tool. It can be selected from the Options bar, or by clicking and holding on the black triangle in the corner of the Clone Stamp tool and then selecting the Pattern Stamp tool from the subsequent list.

Hot tip

Patterns can be added to the patterns panel by selecting an image, or an area of an image, and selecting Edit> Define Pattern from the Editor Menu bar. Then give the pattern a name in the Pattern Name dialog box and click OK.

Healing Brush

One of the favorite techniques in digital imaging is removing unwanted items, particularly physical blemishes, such as spots and wrinkles. This can be done with the Clone tool but the effects can sometimes be too harsh, as a single area is copied over the affected item. A more subtle effect can be achieved with the Healing Brush and the Spot Healing Brush tools. The Healing Brush can be used to remove blemishes over larger areas, such as wrinkles:

1 Open an image with blemishes covering a reasonably large area, i.e. more than a single spot

2 Select the Healing Brush tool from the Toolbox and make the required selections in the Options bar

3 Hold down Alt and click on an area of the image to load the Healing Brush tool. Drag over the affected area. The cross is the area which is copied beneath the circle. At this point the overall tone is not perfect and looks too pink

4 Release the mouse and the Healing Brush blends the affected area with the one that was copied over it. This creates a much more natural skin tone

Hot tip

The Healing Brush tool is more subtle than the Clone tool, as it blends the copied area together with the area over which it is copying. This is particularly effective on people, as it preserves the overall skin tone better than the Clone tool does.

Spot Healing Brush

The Spot Healing Brush is very effective for quickly removing small blemishes in an image, such as spots. To do this:

1 Open an image and zoom in on the area with the blemish

Hot tip

When dragging over a blemish with the Spot Healing Brush tool, make sure the brush size is larger than the area of the blemish. This will ensure that you can cover the blemish in a single stroke.

2 Select the Spot Healing Brush tool from the Toolbox and make the required selections in the Options bar

3 Drag the Spot Healing Brush tool over the affected area

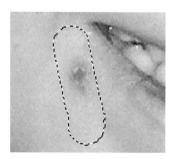

4 The blemish is removed and the overall skin tone is retained

Rotating

Various rotation commands can be applied to images, and also individual layers in layered images. This can be useful for positioning items and also for correcting the orientation of an image that is on its side or upside down.

Rotating a whole image

Hot tip

If an image is only slightly misaligned, then only a small angle figure is required in the Rotate Canvas dialog box. A figure of 1 or 2 can sometimes be sufficient.

1 Select Image>Rotate from the Menu bar

2 Select a rotation option from the menu

3 Select Custom to enter your own value for the amount you want an image rotated

4 Click on the OK button

Rotating a layer

To rotate separate layers within an image:

Don't forget

For more information about working with layers, see Chapter Seven.

1 Open an image that consists of two or more layers. Select one of the layers in the Layers panel

2 Select Image>Rotate from the Menu bar

3 Select a layer rotation option from the menu

4 The selected layer is rotated independently

Transforming

The Transform commands can be used to resize an image, and to apply some basic distortion techniques. These commands can be accessed by selecting Image>Transform from the Menu bar.

Free Transform

This enables you to manually alter the size and shape of an image. To do this:

1 Select Image>Transform>Free Transform from the Menu bar

2 Click and drag here to transform the vertical and horizontal size of the image. Hold down Shift to transform it in proportion

Don't forget

The other options from the Transform menu are Skew, Distort and Perspective. These can be accessed and applied in a similar way to the Free Transform option.

Magnification

There are a number of ways in Elements in which the magnification at which an image is being viewed can be increased or decreased. This can be useful if you want to zoom in on a particular part of an image, for editing purposes, or if you want to view a whole image to see the result of editing effects that have been applied.

View menu

1 Select View from the Menu bar and select one of the options from the View menu

Zoom tool

1 Select the Zoom tool from the Toolbox

2 Click once on an image to enlarge it (usually by 100% each time). Hold down Alt and click to decrease the magnification

Navigator panel

This can be used to move around an image and also magnify certain areas. To use the Navigator panel:

1 Access the Navigator panel by selecting Window>Navigator from the Menu bar

2 Drag this slider to magnify the area of the image within the red rectangle

Don't forget

The Navigator also has buttons for zooming in and out. These are located at the left and right of the slider.

69

3 Drag the rectangle to change the area of the image that is being magnified

Eraser

The Eraser tool can be used to remove areas of an image. In a simple, single layer image, this can just leave a blank hole, which has to be filled with something. The Eraser options are:

1   Eraser, which can be used to erase part of the background image or a layer within it

2   Background Eraser, which can be used to remove an uneven background

3   Magic Eraser, which can be used to quickly remove a solid background (see below)

Erasing a background

With the Magic Eraser tool, it is possible to delete a colored background in an image. To do this:

1   Open an image with an evenly colored background

2   Select the Magic Eraser and make the required selections in the Options bar. Make sure the Contiguous box is not checked

3   Click once on the background. It is removed from the image, regardless of where it occurs

4 Quick Wins

In digital image editing there are a number of techniques that can be used to significantly enhance almost every image, from improving the color to whitening teeth. This chapter looks at some of these "quick wins" and shows how they can be used to improve the visual impact of images.

Removing Red-eye

One of the most common problems with photographs of people, whether they are taken digitally or with a film-based camera, is red-eye. This is caused when the camera's flash is used and then reflects in the subject's pupils. This can create the dreaded red-eye effect, when the subject can unintentionally be transformed into a demonic character. Unless you have access to professional studio lighting equipment, or have a removable flash unit that can be positioned away from the subject's face, sooner or later you will capture images that contain red-eye.

Elements has recognized that removing red-eye is one of the top priorities for most amateur photographers and a specific tool for this purpose has been included in the Toolbox: the Red Eye Removal tool. To use this:

Hot tip

The best way to deal with red-eye is to avoid it in the first place. Try using a camera that has a red-eye reduction function. This uses an extra flash, just before the picture is taken, to diminish the effect of red-eye.

1 Open an image that contains red-eye

2 Select the Zoom tool from the Toolbox

72

3 Drag around the affected area until it appears at a suitable magnification

4 Select the Red Eye Removal tool from the Toolbox

5 Click in the Options bar to select the size of the pupil and the amount by which it will be darkened

| Pupil Size: 50% | Darken Amount: 50% | Auto |

6 Click once on the red-eye, or drag around the affected area

7 The red-eye is removed

73

Adjusting Skin Tones

Skin tone can sometimes cause problems in digital images. At times they can look washed-out and pale or contain a slightly unnatural color cast. This can be edited with the Adjust Skin Tones function, which can be used to improve the skin tone of a pale image, or just to give someone a more tanned or healthy appearance. To do this:

74

1 In the Editor, open an image whose skin tone you want to adjust

2 Select Enhance> Adjust Color> Adjust Color for Skin Tone from the Menu bar

3 Click on the image to automatically adjust the skin tone in relation to the selected area

4 Drag these sliders to alter the amount of tan and blush in the skin tone

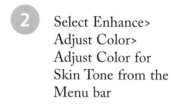

5 Drag this slider to edit the overall light in the image

6 Click on the OK button

Straightening an Image

If you use scanned images, you will quickly discover that it can be difficult to capture a perfectly straight image. Invariably, scanned images appear at a slight angle once the scanning process has been completed, however careful you are when you place the original image in the scanner. As shown in Chapter Three, images can be rotated manually, but there is also a function for straightening images in one operation. To straighten an image:

Hot tip

When scanning images it is best not to spend too much time trying to get the image straight. This is because it can be a frustrating process and also because of the ease with which Elements can cure the problem.

1 Open the image that requires to be straightened

Don't forget

Once they have been straightened, images can also be cropped manually using the Crop tool in the Toolbox.

2 Select the Straighten tool from the Toolbox:

3 Drag on the image at the angle by which you want it to be straightened

Don't forget

Images can also be straightened by selecting Image> Rotate>Straighten and Crop Image from the Menu bar.

4 The image is straightened according to the angle used in Step 3

Dividing Scanned Images

Scanning is now a very popular way to capture digital images by converting existing hard copy photographs. Previously, each image had to be scanned individually, or several images could be scanned at the same time but they then had to be copied and cropped individually, which could be a tedious process. However, it is now possible to take the hard work out of dividing scanned images by letting Elements do it automatically. To do this:

Beware

When scanning images to be divided, make sure that there is enough white space between them and that each image has a clearly defined border. This will enable Elements to clearly identify the separate images and then divide them.

 Scan two, or more, images at the same time

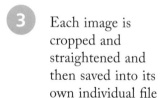 Select Image>Divide Scanned Photos from the Menu bar

 Each image is cropped and straightened and then saved into its own individual file

Quick Edit Options

The Quick Edit options in Elements offer a number of functions within the one location. This makes it easier to apply a number of techniques at the same time.

Using Quick Edit

1 Open an image in the Editor and click on the Edit Quick button

2 Click here for options on how the image is displayed on screen

3 Click here for options for zooming, moving around the image and cropping

4 Correction panels are located here. Click a right-pointing arrow to expand a panel

5 Click here to specify how the editing changes are displayed

...cont'd

Smart Fix

This performs several editing changes in a single operation. Click on the Auto button to have the changes applied automatically, or drag the slider to specify the amount of the editing changes.

Don't forget

Changes are displayed in the main Quick Fix window as they are being made.

Lighting Fixes

This provides options for adjusting the lighting and contrast in an image. Click on the Auto buttons to adjust the lighting range within an image and the contrast. Drag the sliders to adjust the lightest, darkest and midtone areas within an image.

Don't forget

In general, when applying lighting fixes, it is more effective to apply them manually rather than using the Auto functions.

Color Fixes

Click on the Auto button to adjust the hue and saturation in an image, or drag the sliders to make manual adjustments.

Balance Fixes

Drag the sliders to adjust the warmth of the colors in an image and the color balance.

Detail Fixes

This can be used to apply sharpening to an image to make it clearer, either automatically with the Auto button or manually with the slider.

Touch Up Quick Edits

Touch Up Quick Edits provide options for performing tasks, such as whitening teeth and brightening dull skies. To access the Touch Up Quick Edits, click here in the Quick Edit panel.

Brightening dull skies
To make dull skies appear brighter:

The Make Dull Skies Blue tool applies the effect to everything in the selection. This can result in clouds taking on a bluish tinge.

Beware

80

1. Open an image with a sky you want to brighten

2. Click on the Make Dull Skies Blue tool

3. Drag the tool over the area of the sky you want to brighten. As you drag, the area will become selected and automatically brightened

Whitening teeth

Everyone likes to see white teeth in a photo, and with the teeth whitening tool this is possible for anyone. To do this:

1 Open an image and click on the Whiten Teeth tool

2 Click on the Zoom tool

3 Drag the Zoom tool around the teeth area

Hot tip

Apply the Whiten Teeth effect more than once if you want to get really sparkling teeth.

4 Click here to select a brush size for the Whiten Teeth tool

5 Drag the Whiten Teeth tool over the teeth

6 The teeth area is selected and whitened in one operation

81

Cleaning Up Scenes

When taking photos of people a common problem is that unwanted objects appear in the background, particularly moving objects such as other people or vehicles. In Elements there is a Scene Cleaner function that enables you to remove these unwanted objects, so that you end up with exactly the composition that you want. To do this:

1 Open two, or more, images in the Editor with unwanted elements in the background

82

2 Select File>New>Photomerge Scene Cleaner from the Menu bar

3 One image is shown in the left-hand panel of the Scene Cleaner. This is the source image for the final one

4 Drag another image into the right-hand panel. This will form the basis of the final image

5 Click on the Pencil tool

6 Drag the Pencil tool over the area you want removed in the final image. The corresponding area is copied from the source image

Don't forget

You can also drag the Pencil tool over a clear area in the source image and this will copy over the equivalent area in the final image.

7 Add any areas to the selection. Once you have finished drawing, the corresponding area from the source image will cover this area in the final image

8 Click on the Done button

Done

9 The unwanted elements are removed from the image and it can be saved in the usual way

Merging Exposures

A fundamental element of photography is getting the correct exposure, i.e. the right amount of light to make all parts of an image look at their best. Sometimes images are under-exposed (too dark) or over-exposed (too light). However, Elements has a function that can combine the exposures in separate images to provide a correctly exposed final image. To do this it is best to capture the same scene at different exposures.

Hot tip

The merge exposure feature works best when you have two identical images (such as a landscape) at different exposures. This can be done by using a tripod when capturing the source images.

84

1. Open an image that is under-exposed (too dark)

2. Open an image that is over-exposed (too light). Select both of the images in the Project Bin

3. Select File>New>Photomerge Exposure from the Menu bar. This accesses the Photomerge window

4 Click on the Automatic tab to have the exposure corrected in one click. Click on Simple Blending for the exposures to be merged automatically. Click on Smart Blending to have more control by using the sliders

With the Automatic Photomerge Exposure option you can copy an element from one image into another. With the Manual option the two images are merged together to give a better, overall, exposure.

5 Click on the Manual tab to merge different elements of the two images. Use the Selection Tool to draw on an element of one of the images that you want to appear on the final image

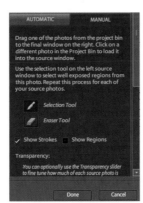

6 Click on the Done button to create the merged image

7 A composite image is created from the two original ones. Save this using a new file name

Changing to Black and White

Most digital cameras and scanners are capable of converting color images into black and white at the point of capture. However, it is also possible to use Elements to convert existing color images into black and white ones. To do this:

When creating black and white images, make a copy of the original first. Use the copy to create the new image.

1 Open a color image and select Enhance> Convert to Black and White from the Menu bar

2 The Convert to Black and White dialog box has various options for how the image is converted

3 Select the type of black and white effect to be applied, depending on the subject in the image

Select a style:

- Infrared Effect
- Newspaper
- **Portraits**
- Scenic Landscape
- Urban/Snapshots
- Vivid Landscapes

4 Drag these sliders to specify the intensity of the effect to be applied for different elements

Adjust Intensity:

Red: – ———————— +
Green: – ———————— +
Blue: – ———————— +
Contrast: – ———————— +

5 Click on the OK button

OK

6 The image is converted into black and white, according to the settings that have been selected

Hot tip

A similar effect can be achieved by selecting Enhance>Adjust Color>Remove Color from the Menu bar.

Combining Group Shots

Group shots are one of the most common uses for digital photography, but they can also be one of the most frustrating: in any group there is usually someone who is looking the wrong way or blinking. In Elements there is a Photomerge function that can ensure you always get people looking their best in a group shot. It does this by combining the best parts from different images. To do this:

1 Select two or more images in the Project Bin

2 Select File>New>Photomerge Group Shot from the Menu bar

3 The current source file is shown on the left in the Group Shot window

Hot tip

If you want to change the positions of the Source and Final images, re-order them in the Editor's Project Bin by dragging them.

4 Drag one of the images from the Project Bin into the right-hand panel in the Group Shot window. This is the image that will be the basis of the final image

5   Select the Pencil Tool in the Group Shot window

6   On the Source file, draw around the areas which you want copied into the final image. This can include faces of people, and also whole people, who may have been left out of one of the original shots

Hot tip

This process can also be used to copy other items into an image, such as objects and buildings, not just people.

7   The selection in Step 6 is copied to the final, destination image

8   Click on the Done button to save the composite image as a new file

Done

Combining Faces

As well as being able to combine different group shots, it is also possible to combine different elements of people's faces together. To do this:

1 Select two or more images in the Project Bin

2 Select File>New>Photomerge Faces from the Menu bar

3 The current source file is shown on the left in the Group Shot window

Don't forget

Combining face elements works best with two subjects who have features of roughly the same size.

4 Drag one of the images from the Project Bin into the right-hand panel in the Faces window. This is the image that will be the basis of the final image

5 In the Faces window, click on the Alignment Tool. This will be used to ensure both images are at the same size and orientation

Alignment Tool

6 Align the three markers over the eyes and nose of the source image

7 Align the three markers over the eyes and nose of the source image in the Final window

8 Click on the Align Photos button

9 The photos are displayed at the same size and orientation

Don't forget

Use the Zoom tool in the Photomerge Faces window to increase the size of each subject. This is done simultaneously for both.

10 Click on the Pencil Tool button

11 Draw over the required elements in the source image

12 The selected area in Step 11 is copied to the final, destination photo

13 Click on the Done button to save the composite image as a new file

Panoramas

Creating panoramas

For anyone who takes landscape pictures, the desire to create a panorama occurs sooner or later. With film-based cameras, this usually involves sticking several photographs together to create the panorama, albeit a rather patchwork one. With digital images the end result can look a lot more professional and Elements has a dedicated function for achieving this: Photomerge.

When creating a panorama there are a few rules to follow:

- If possible, use a tripod to ensure that your camera stays at the same level for all of the shots

- Keep the same exposure settings for all images

- Make sure that there is a reasonable overlap between images (about 20%). Some cameras enable you to align the correct overlap between the images

- Keep the same distance between yourself and the object you are capturing. Otherwise the end result will look out of perspective

To create a panorama:

Beware

Do not include too many images in a panorama, otherwise it could be too large for viewing or printing easily.

1 Select File>New>Photomerge Panorama from the Menu bar

2 Select an option for the type of panorama image that you want to create

3 Click on the Browse button to locate images you want to use on your computer

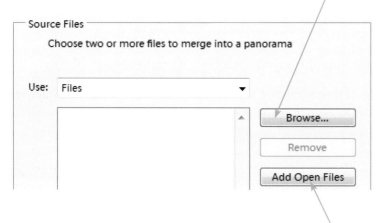

Source Files

Choose two or more files to merge into a panorama

Use: Files

Browse...

Remove

Add Open Files

4 Or, click on the Add Open Files button to use images that are already open

5 If you Browse for images, select them from your computer

DSC_0449   DSC_0450   DSC_0451

6 Click on the OK button   OK

...cont'd

7 In some instances the final image may need some additional editing. One common problem is the appearance of diagonal lines across the image, particularly in the sky region

8 Panoramas can usually be improved by applying color correction such as Brightness/Contrast and Shadows/Highlights. They can also be cropped to straighten the borders

9 An unwanted line in a panorama can be removed by cloning from a nearby area, or by selecting it and applying color correction until it is the same tone as the rest of the image. Some trial and error may be needed to achieve exactly the right look

5 Beyond the Basics

Since Elements is based on the full version of Photoshop, it contains a number of powerful features for precise image editing. This chapter looks at some of these features and shows how you can use them to take your image editing skills to the next level.

Hue and Saturation

The hue and saturation command can be used to edit the color elements of an image. However, it works slightly differently from other commands, such as those for the brightness and contrast. There are three areas that are covered by the hue and saturation command: color, color strength and lightness. To adjust the hue and saturation of an image:

1 Open an image

2 Select Enhance> Adjust Color>Adjust Hue/Saturation

Hot tip

By altering the hue of an image, some interesting abstract color effects can be created. This can be very effective if you are producing several versions of the same image, such as for an artistic poster.

96

3 Drag this slider to adjust the hue of the image, i.e. change the colors in the image

Don't forget

Hue is used to describe the color of a particular pixel or an image.

4 Drag this slider to adjust the saturation, i.e. the intensity of colors in the image

Don't forget

The Lightness option is similar to adjusting image brightness.

5 Check on the Colorize box to color the image with the hue of the currently selected foreground color in the Color Picker, which is located at the bottom of the Toolbox

Hot tip

The Colorize option can be used to create some interesting "color wash" effects. Try altering the Hue slider once the Colorize box has been checked on.

Don't forget

For more on working with color and the Color Picker, see Chapter Eight.

6 Click on the OK button to apply any changes that have been made

Histogram

The histogram is a device that displays the tonal range of the pixels in an image, and it can be used for very precise editing of an image. The histogram (Window>Histogram) is depicted in a graph format and it displays how the pixels in an image are distributed across the image, from the darkest (black) to the lightest (white) points. Another way of considering the histogram is that it displays the values of an image's highlights, midtones and shadows:

Don't forget

The histogram works by looking at the individual color channels of an image (Red, Green, Blue, also known as the RGB color model) or at a combination of all three, which is displayed as the Luminosity in the Channel box. It can also look at all of the colors in an image.

Highlights

Midtones

Shadows

Don't forget

Image formats, such as JPEG, are edited in Elements using the RGB color model, i.e. red, green and blue mixed together to create the colors in the image.

Highlights

Midtones

Shadows

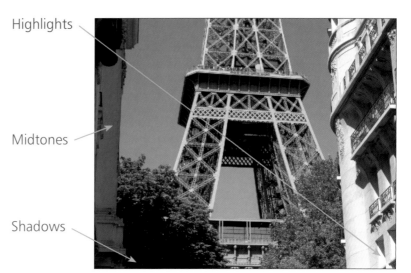

Ideally, the histogram graph should show a reasonably consistent range of tonal distribution, indicating an image that has good contrast and detail:

However, if the tonal range is bunched at one end of the graph, this indicates that the image is under-exposed or over-exposed:

Hot tip

If the histogram is left open, it will update automatically as editing changes are made to an image. This gives a good idea of how effective the changes are.

Over-exposure

Under-exposure

Levels

While the histogram displays the tonal range of an image, the Levels function can be used to edit this range. Any changes made using the Levels function will then be visible in the histogram. Levels allow you to redistribute pixels between the darkest and lightest points in an image, and also to set these points manually if you want to. To use the Levels function:

The Levels function can be used to adjust the tonal range of a specific area of an image, by first making a selection and then using the Levels dialog box. For more details on selecting areas see Chapter Six.

Don't forget

In the Levels dialog box, the graph is the same as the one shown in the histogram.

Open an image

Select Enhance>Adjust Lighting>Levels from the Menu bar

Don't forget

Image shadows, midtones and highlights can be altered by dragging the markers for the black, midtone and white input points.

Midtone input point

Black input point

White input point

Output points

3 Drag the black point and the white point sliders to, or beyond, the first pixels denoted in the graph to increase the contrast

Don't forget

It is worth adjusting an image's black and white points before any other editing is performed.

Hot tip

Move the midtones point slider to darken or lighten the midtones in an image.

4 Drag the output sliders towards the middle to decrease the contrast

Don't forget

The Auto button, in the Levels dialog box, produces the same effect as using the Enhance>Auto Levels command from the Menu bar.

101

Color Curves

Another option for editing the colors in an image is the Color Curves function. This enables different elements of an image to be edited within the same dialog window and it offers great variety for editing several different elements of an image. To do this:

1 Open an image

2 Select Enhance>Adjust Color>Adjust Color Curves from the Menu bar

3 Click on one of the styles for how the Color Curves are applied to the selected image

4 Drag these sliders to adjust the highlights, brightness, contrast and shadows in the image

Hot tip

Using the Color Curves graph takes a bit of experimentation, but it can be an excellent way to subtly alter the color in an image.

5 Click and drag on the graph to alter the color within the image

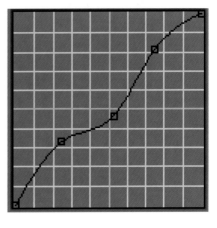

Pegging Points

Since Levels works by distributing pixels between the black and white points of an image, it makes sense to define these points for each image. This can be done by using the eyedroppers in the Levels dialog box:

1 With an image open, access the Levels dialog box by selecting Enhance>Adjust Lighting>Levels from the Menu bar

2 Click on the Set Black Point eyedropper and click on the image's darkest point to set the black point

3 Click on the Set Gray Point eyedropper and click on a gray area to set the midtone point

4 Click on the Set White Point eyedropper and click on the image's lightest point to set the white point

Hot tip

The Info panel can be used to see the color values of the areas selected for the black, white and gray points.

Hot tip

To set a white point, use an area that is colored white, rather than a burnt out area of an image, i.e. one that is too over-exposed.

Don't forget

If the color in an image does not look right after setting the black, gray and white points, try selecting different areas of color with the relevant eyedroppers.

Filter Adjustments

There are numerous special effects within the Artworks and Filters panel. However, there are also some filter effects that can be used to alter the color in the image. These are known as filter adjustment effects. To use these:

1 Open an image and select Filter>Adjustments from the Menu bar

2 Select either Equalize, Invert or Posterize

Equalize

Invert

Posterize

Unsharp Mask

Although sharpening is a useful technique for improving the overall definition of an image, it can sometimes appear too harsh and "jaggy". For a more subtle effect, the Unsharp Mask can be used. This works by increasing the contrast between light and dark pixels in an image. To use the Unsharp Mask:

1 Open an image that you want to sharpen

2 Select the Enhance> Unsharp Mask option from the Menu bar

Don't forget

The settings for the Unsharp Mask are: Amount, which determines the amount to increase the contrast between pixels; Radius, which determines how many pixels will have the sharpening applied to them in an affected area; Threshold, which determines how different a pixel has to be from its neighbor before sharpening is applied.

3 Apply the appropriate settings in the Unsharp Mask dialog box and click on the OK button

4 The contrast between light and dark pixels is increased, giving the impression of a clearer, or sharper, image

Fixing Camera Distortion

One issue with all cameras is that objects can sometimes appear distorted, particularly if they are not in the center of the frame. This is because of the curved nature of a camera lens: this curvature can make objects appear bent. However, Elements has a function for fixing camera distortion when it appears. To do this:

1 Open an image where an object appears distorted and bent

2 Select Filter>Correct Camera Distortion from the Menu bar

Hot tip

To check the level of distortion for your camera, take photos with an object or a building at the side of the frame and also in the center. Also, try capturing it from different distances to see how this affects the overall distortion.

3 The Correct Camera Distortion window contains the tools for correcting the appearance of bent objects

4 Drag this slider to remove the distortion in the image

5 Drag these sliders to alter the perspective of the image

6 The editing changes are displayed in the Preview window

Beware

When correcting camera distortion for an object in an image, the rest of the image is altered too.

7 Click on the OK button

OK

8 Crop the image as required and save it in the same way as any other image

Importing RAW Images

RAW images are those in which the digital data has not been processed in any way, or converted into any specific file format, by the camera when they were captured. These produce high quality images and are usually available on higher specification digital cameras. However, RAW is becoming more common in consumer digital cameras and they can be downloaded in Elements in the same way as any other image. Once the RAW images are accessed, the Camera Raw dialog box opens so that a variety of editing functions can be applied to the image. RAW images act as a digital negative and have to be saved into another format before they can be used in the conventional way. To edit RAW images:

Beware

RAW images are much larger in file size than the same versions captured as JPEGs.

Don't forget

The RAW format should be used if you want to make manual changes to an image to achieve the highest possible quality.

 Open a RAW image in the Editor or from the Organizer

 In the Camera RAW dialog box, editing functions that are usually performed when an image is captured, can be made manually

 Click here to adjust the White Balance in the image

 Drag these sliders to adjust the Color Temperature and Tint in the image

5 Drag these sliders to adjust the Exposure, Shadows, Brightness, Contrast and Saturation in the image

6 Click on the Detail tab and drag these sliders to adjust the Sharpness and Noise in the image

7 Click on the Open Image button. This opens the image in Full Edit mode, from where it can also be saved as a standard file format, such as JPEG

Open Image

Image Size

The physical size of a digital image can sometimes be a confusing issue, as it is frequently dealt with under the term "resolution". Unfortunately, resolution can be applied to a number of areas of digital imaging: image resolution, monitor resolution, print size and print resolution.

Image resolution

The resolution of an image is determined by the number of pixels in it. This is counted as a vertical and a horizontal value, e.g. 3000 x 2000. When multiplied together it gives the overall resolution, i.e. 6,000,000 pixels in this case. This is frequently the headline figure quoted by digital camera manufacturers, e.g. 6 million pixels (or 6 megapixels). To view the image resolution in Elements:

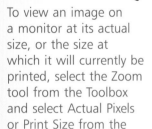

Hot tip

To view an image on a monitor at its actual size, or the size at which it will currently be printed, select the Zoom tool from the Toolbox and select Actual Pixels or Print Size from the Options bar.

1 Select Image>Resize>Image Size from the Menu bar

2 The image size is displayed here (in pixels)

Don't forget

The Resolution figure under the Document Size heading is used to determine the size at which the image will be printed. If this is set to 72 pixels/inch, then the onscreen size and the printed size should be roughly the same.

Monitor resolution

Most modern computer monitors display digital images at between 72 and 96 pixels per inch (ppi). This means that every inch of the screen contains approximately this number of pixels. So, for an image being displayed at 100%, the onscreen size will be the number of pixels horizontally divided by 72 (or 96 depending on the monitor) and the same vertically. In the above example, this would mean the image would be viewed at 39 inches by 59 inches approximately (2848/72 and 4272/72) on a monitor. In modern web browsers this is usually adjusted so that the whole image is accommodated on the viewable screen.

Document size (print resolution)

Pixels in an image are not a set size, which means that images can be printed in a variety of sizes, simply by contracting or expanding the available pixels. This is done by changing the resolution in the Document Size section of the Image Size dialog box. (When dealing with document size, think of this as the size of the printed document.) To set the size at which an image will be printed:

1. Select Image>Resize>Image Size from the Menu bar

2. Change the resolution here (or change the Width and Height of the document size). Make sure the Resample Image box is not checked

3. By changing one value, the other two are updated too. Click on the OK button

Hot tip

The higher the print resolution, the better the final printed image. Aim for a minimum of 200 pixels per inch for the best printed output.

Hot tip

To work out the size at which an image will be printed, divide the pixel dimensions (height and width) by the resolution value under the Document Size heading.

Don't forget

The print resolution determines how many pixels are used in each inch of the printed image (ppi). However, the number of colored dots used to represent each pixel on the paper is determined by the printer resolution, measured in dots per inch (dpi). So if the print resolution is 72 ppi and the printer resolution is 2880 dpi, each pixel will be represented by 40 colored dots, i.e. 2880 divided by 72.

111

Resampling Images

All digital images can be increased or decreased in size. This involves adding or removing pixels from the image. Decreasing the size of an image is relatively straightforward and involves removing redundant pixels. However, increasing the size of an image involves adding pixels by digital guesswork. To do this, Elements looks at the existing pixels and works out the nearest match for the ones that are to be added. Increasing or decreasing the size of a digital image is known as "resampling".

Resampling

Resampling down decreases the size of the image and it is more effective than resampling up. To do this:

1. Select Image> Resize>Image Size from the Menu bar

2. Check the Resample Image box

3. Resample the image by changing the pixel dimensions, the height and width or the resolution

4. Changing any of the values above alters the physical size of the image. Click on the OK button

6 Selecting Areas

The true power of digital image editing comes into its own when you are able to select areas of an image and edit them independently. This chapter looks at the various ways that selections can be made and edited within Elements.

About Selections

One of the most important aspects of image editing is the ability to select areas within an image. This can be used in a number of different ways:

- Selecting an object to apply an editing technique to it (such as changing the brightness or contrast) without affecting the rest of the image

- Selecting a particular color in an image

- Selecting an area to apply a special effect to it

- Selecting an area to remove it

Elements has several tools that can be used to select items, and there are also a number of editing functions that can be applied to selections.

Two examples of how selections can be used are:

114

1   Select an area within an image and delete it

2   Select an area and add a color or special effect

Marquee Tools

There are two options for the Marquee tool: the Rectangular Marquee tool and the Elliptical Marquee tool. Both of these can be used to make symmetrical selections. To use the Marquee tools:

1 Select either the Rectangular or the Elliptical Marquee tool from the Toolbox. Select the required options from the Options bar

2 Make a symmetrical selection with one of the tools by clicking and dragging on an image

Don't forget

To access additional tools from the Toolbox, click and hold on the black triangle next to one of the default tools, and select one of the subsequent options that are available.

Hot tip

To make a selection that is exactly square or round, hold down Shift when dragging with the Rectangular Marquee tool or the Elliptical Marquee tool respectively.

Elliptical selection   Rectangular selection

Lasso Tools

There are three options for the Lasso tools, which can be used to make freehand selections. To use these:

Lasso tool

 Select the Lasso tool from the Toolbox and select the required options from the Options bar

 Make a freehand selection by clicking and dragging around an object

Polygonal Lasso tool

Select the Polygonal Lasso tool from the Toolbox and select the required options from the Options bar

Make a selection by clicking on specific points around an object, and then dragging to the next point

Magnetic Lasso tool

1 Select the Magnetic Lasso tool from the Toolbox and select the required options from the Options bar

2 Click once on an image to create the first anchor point

3 Make a selection by dragging continuously around an object. The selection line snaps to the closest strongest edge, i.e. the one with the most contrast. Fastening points are added as the selection is made

Magic Wand Tool

The Magic Wand tool can be used to select areas of the same, or similar, color. To do this:

1 Select the Magic Wand tool from the Toolbox and select the required options from the Options bar

Tolerance: 32 ✓ Anti-alias ✓ Contiguous ☐ All Layers

2 Click on a color to select all of the adjacent pixels that are the same, or similar, color, depending on the options selected from the Options bar

Selection Brush Tool

The Selection Brush tool can be used to select areas by using a brush-like stroke. Unlike with the Marquee or Lasso tools, the area selected by the Selection Brush tool is the one directly below where the tool moves. To make a selection with the Selection Brush tool:

1 Select the Selection Brush tool from the Toolbox and select the required options from the Options bar

Don't forget

The Selection Brush tool can be used to select an area, or to mask an area. This can be determined in the Mode box in the Options bar.

2 Click and drag to make a selection

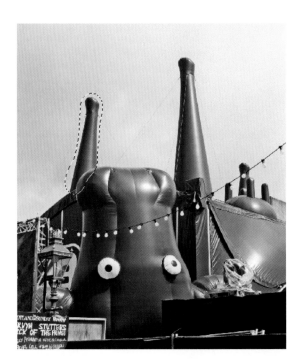

3 The selection area is underneath the borders of the Selection Brush tool

Quick Selection Tool

The Quick Selection tool can be used to select areas of similar color by drawing over the general area, without having to make a specific selection. To do this:

1 Select the Quick Selection tool from the Toolbox

2 Select the required options from the Options bar

3 Draw over an area, or part of an area, to select all of the similarly colored pixels

Smart Brush Tool

The Smart Brush tool can be used to quickly select large areas in an image (in a similar way to the Quick Selection tool) and then have effects applied automatically to the selected area. To do this:

1 Open the image to which you want to apply changes with the Smart Brush tool

2 Select the Smart Brush tool from the Toolbox

3 Select the editing effect you want to apply to the area selected by the Smart Brush tool, from the Options bar

4 Select Brush size for the Smart Brush tool, from the Options bar

5 Drag the Smart Brush tool over an area of the image. In the left-hand image, below, the building has been selected and brightened, in the right-hand image the sky has been selected and enhanced

Inverting a Selection

This can be a useful option if you have edited a selection and then want to edit the rest of the image without affecting the area you have just selected. To do this:

1 Make a selection

2 Choose Select> Inverse from the Menu bar

3 The selection becomes inverted, i.e. if a background object was selected the foreground is now selected

Feathering

Feathering is a technique that can be used to soften the edges of a selection by making them slightly blurry. This can be used if you are pasting a selection into another image, or if you want to soften the edges around a portrait of an individual. To do this:

Don't forget

Feathering can also be selected from the Options bar once a Marquee tool is selected, and before the selection has been made.

1. Make a selection

2. Choose Select> Feather from the Menu bar

3. Enter a Feather value (the number of pixels around the radius of the selection

that will be blurred). Click on the OK button

Hot tip

If required, crop the final image so that the feathered subject is more prominent.

4. Invert the selection, as shown on the previous page, and delete the background by pressing Delete. This will leave the selection around the subject with softened edges

Editing Selections

When you have made a selection, you can edit it in a number of ways.

Moving a selection
Make a selection and select the Move tool from the Toolbox. Drag the selection to move it to a new location.

Changing the selection area
Make a selection with a selection tool. With the same tool selected, click and drag within the selection area to move it over another part of the image.

Adding to a selection
Make a selection and click on this button in the Options bar. Make another selection to create a single larger selection. The two selections do not have to intersect.

Intersecting with a selection
To create a selection by intersecting two existing selections: make a selection and click on this button in the Options bar. Make another selection that intersects the first. The intersected area will become the selection.

Expanding a selection
To expand a selection by a specific number of pixels: make a selection and choose Select>Modify>Expand from the Menu bar. In the Expand Selection dialog box, enter the amount by which you want the selection expanded.

Growing a selection
The Grow command can be used on a selection when it has been made with the Magic Wand tool, and some of the pixels within the selection have been omitted. To do this:

Make a selection with the Magic Wand tool and make the required choices from the Options bar. Choose Select>Grow from the Menu bar. Depending on the choices in the Options bar, the omitted pixels will be included in the selection.

7 Layers

Layers provide the means to add numerous elements to an image, and edit them independently from one another. This chapter looks at how to use layers to expand your creative possibilities.

Layering Images

Layering is a technique that enables you to add additional elements to an image, and place them on separate layers, so that they can be edited and manipulated independently from other elements in the image. It is like creating an image using transparent sheets of film: each layer is independent of the others but, when they are combined, a composite image is created. This is an extremely versatile technique for working with digital images.

By using layers, several different elements can be combined to create a composite image:

Original image

Final image
With text and a shape added (two additional layers have been added).

Layers Panel

The use of layers within Elements is governed by the Layers panel. When an image is first opened it is shown in the Layers panel as the Background layer. While this remains as the Background layer it cannot be moved above any other layers. However, it can be converted into a normal layer, in which case it operates in the same way as any other layer. To convert a Background layer into a normal one:

1 The open image is shown in the Layers panel as the Background

2 Double-click here

Hot tip

The Background layer can also be converted into a normal one by applying certain editing functions to the image. These are the Background Eraser tool, the Magic Eraser tool and the Red-Eye Removal tool.

3 Enter a name for the layer and click on the OK button

4 The Background layer is converted into a normal layer in the Layers panel

Don't forget

The Layers panel menu can be accessed by clicking on the More button at the top right of the Layers panel.

Adding Layers

New blank layers can be added whenever you want to include new content within an image. This could be part of another image that has been copied and pasted, a whole new image, text or an object. To add a new layer:

Don't forget

Text is automatically added on a new layer within an image.

1 Click here on the Layers panel

Don't forget

To edit an item on a particular layer, first make sure that the correct layer is selected in the Layers panel. A selected layer is known as the active layer and it is highlighted in the Layers panel with a solid color through it.

2 Double-click on the layer name and overtype to give the layer a new name

3 With the new layer selected in the Layers panel, add content to the layer. This will be visible over the layer, or layers, below it

Fill and Adjustment Layers

Fill and adjustment layers can be added to images to give an effect behind or above the main subject. To do this:

1 Open the Layers panel and select a layer. The fill or adjustment layer will be placed directly above the selected layer

2 Click here at the bottom of the Layers panel

3 Select one of the fill or adjustment options. The fill options are Solid Color, Gradient or Pattern Fill

Solid Color...
Gradient...
Pattern...

Levels...
Brightness/Contrast...

Hue/Saturation...
Gradient Map...
Photo Filter...

Invert
Threshold...
Posterize...

129

Beware

For a Fill layer to be visible behind the main image, the image must have a transparent background. To achieve this, select the main subject. Choose Select>Inverse from the Menu bar and press the Delete key to delete the background. A checkerboard effect should be visible, which denotes that this part of the image is transparent. This only works on layers that have been converted into normal layers, rather than the Background one.

Don't forget

The Adjustments panel is used for Levels, Brightness/Contrast, Hue/Saturation, Gradient Map, Photo Filter, Threshold and Posterize.

...cont'd

4 For a Solid Color, Gradient or Pattern Fill, the required fill is selected from a dialog box and this is added to the selected layer

5 For an adjustment option, settings can be applied within the Adjustments panel

6 Once fill and adjustment settings have been applied, the effect can be edited by changing the opacity. This is done by dragging this slider

7 The opacity level determines how much of the image is visible through the fill or adjustment layer

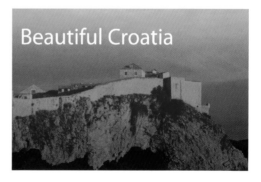

Working with Layers

Moving layers

The order in which layers are arranged in the Layers panel is known as the stacking order. It is possible to change a layer's position in the stacking order, which affects how it is viewed in the composite image. To do this:

1 Click and drag a layer within the Layers panel to change its stacking order

Hiding layers

Layers can be hidden while you are working on other parts of an image. However, the layer is still part of the composite image – it has not been removed. To hide a layer:

1 Click here so that the eye icon disappears. Click again to reveal it

Locking layers

Layers can be locked, so that they cannot accidentally be edited while you are working on other parts of an image. To do this:

1 Select a layer and click here so that a padlock appears next to it

Blending Layers

Blending is a technique that enables two layers to interact with each other in a variety of ways. To do this:

1 Select a layer, either in the Layers panel or by clicking on the relevant item within an image

2 Click here on the Layers panel

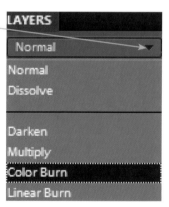

3 Select a blend option

4 The selected blend option determines how the selected layer interacts with the one below

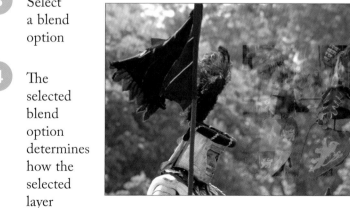

Opacity

The opacity of a layer can be set to determine how much of the layer below is visible through the selected layer. To do this:

1 Select a layer either in the Layers panel or by clicking on the relevant item within an image

2 Click here and drag the slider to achieve the required

level of opacity. The greater the amount of opacity, the less transparent the selected layer becomes

3 The opacity setting determines how much of the background, or the layer below, is visible through the selected one and this can be used to create some interesting artistic effects, including a watermark effect if the opacity is applied to a single layer with nothing behind it

Hot tip

The background behind an image, to which opacity has been applied, can be changed within the Preferences section by selecting Edit>Preferences from the Menu bar and then selecting Transparency and editing the Grid Colors box.

Saving Layers

Once an image has been created using two or more layers, there are two ways in which the composite image can be saved: in a proprietary Photoshop format, in which case individual layers are maintained, or in a general file format, in which case all of the layers will be merged into a single one. The advantage of the former is that individual elements can still be edited within the image, independently of other items. In general, it is good practice to save layered images in both a Photoshop and a non-Photoshop format. To save layered images in a Photoshop format:

Hot tip

Before a layer is saved it is possible to create a composite image consisting of a single layer. To do this, select Layer>Flatten Image from the Menu bar. To merge the existing layer and the one below it, select Layer>Merge Down from the Menu bar, and to merge all visible content (excluding any layers that have been hidden) select Layer> Merge Visible.

1 Select File>Save As from the Menu bar

2 Make sure Photoshop (*.PSD, *.PDD) is selected as the format

3 Make sure the Layers box is checked on

Beware

Layered images that are saved in the Photoshop PSD/PDD format can increase dramatically in file size, compared with the original image or a layered image that has been flattened.

4 Click on the Save button

To save in a non-Photoshop format, select File>Save As from the Menu bar. Select the file format from the Format box and click on the Save button. The Layers box will not be available.

(8) Text and Drawing Tools

Elements offers a lot more than just the ability to edit digital images. It also has options for adding and formatting text and creating a variety of graphical objects. This chapter looks at how to add and edit text and drawing objects.

Adding and Formatting Text

Text can be added to images in Elements and this can be used to create a wide range of items, such as cards, brochures and posters. To add text to an image:

1 Select the Horizontal or Vertical Type tool from the Toolbox

2 Drag on the image with the Type tool to create a text box

3 Make the required formatting selections from the Options bar

Don't forget

Anti-aliasing is a technique that smooths out the jagged edges that can sometimes appear with text when viewed on a computer monitor. Anti-aliasing is created by adding pixels to the edges of text, so that it blends more smoothly with the background.

Font type   Font style Font size   Anti-aliased

Formatting (bold, italic, underline and strikethrough)

Alignment   Spacing   Color   Orientation

Warped text   Text style

4 Type the text onto the image. This is automatically placed on a new layer at the top of the stacking order in the Layers panel

5 To move the text, select it with the Move tool, click and drag it to a new position

To format text that has already been entered:

1 Select a Type tool and drag it over a piece of text to select it

2 Make the changes in the Options bar, as shown in Step 3 on the facing page

Distorting Text

In addition to producing standard text, it is also possible to create some dramatic effects by distorting text. To do this:

1 Enter plain text and select it by dragging a Type tool over it

2 Click the Create Warped Text button on the Options bar

3 Click here and select one of the options in the Warp Text dialog box. Click OK

4 The selected effect is applied to the text

Text and Shape Masks

Text Masks can be used to reveal an area of an image showing through the text. This can be used to produce eye-catching headings and slogans. To do this:

1 Select the Horizontal or Vertical Type Mask tool from the Toolbox

2 Click on an image, enter and format text as you would for normal text. A red mask is applied to the image when the mask text is entered

Hot tip

Text Mask effects work best if the text used is fairly large in size. In some cases it is a good idea to use bold text, as this is wider than standard text.

139

3 Press Enter or click the Move tool to border the mask text with dots

...cont'd

④ Select Edit>Copy from the Menu bar

⑤ Select File>New from the Menu bar and create a new file

⑥ Select Edit>Paste from the Menu bar to paste the text mask into the new file

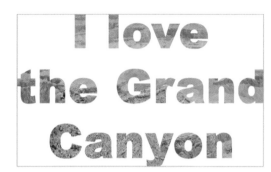

Cookie Cutter masks

A similar effect can be created with shape masks by using the Cookie Cutter tool:

① Select the Cookie Cutter tool in the Toolbox and click here to select a particular style in the Options bar

② Drag on an image to create a cut-out effect

Adding Shapes

Another way to add extra style to your images is through the use of shapes. There are several types of symmetrical shapes that can be added to images, and also a range of custom ones. To add shapes to an image:

1 Click and hold the Rectangle tool in the Toolbox

2 Select the type of shape you want to create

3 Click and drag on the image to create the selected shape

Don't forget

The tools for creating shapes are also available from the Options bar, when the Rectangle tool (or any related tool from this toolset) is selected.

141

4 If you want to change the color of a shape, click here in the Options bar and select a new color. This can either be done before the shape is created or it can be used to edit the color of an existing shape, when selected with the Move tool

...cont'd

Custom shapes

Custom shapes can be used to add pre-designed graphical objects, rather than just symmetrical shapes. To do this:

1 Select the Custom Shape tool from the Toolbox

2 Click here in the Options bar to view the different custom shapes

3 Click once on a shape to select it

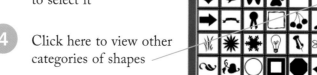

4 Click here to view other categories of shapes

5 Click and drag on an image to add a custom shape

Layer Styles

When plain text and objects are added to images, they appear as two-dimensional items. If you want to give them a 3-D effect, this can be achieved through the use of the Styles and Effects panel.

To do this:

1 Select Window>Effects from the Menu bar

2 Click here to access the Layer Styles

3 Click here to access different styles

Don't forget

Layer Styles can be applied to symmetrical objects and custom ones.

4 Select an object, or a piece of text, with the Move tool and click once on a layer style to apply that style to the selected item in the image

Hot tip

The Drop Shadow styles are a good option for adding emphasis to textual items, such as headings. However, don't over-use them.

Paint Bucket Tool

The Paint Bucket tool can be used to add a solid color to a selection or an object. To do this:

 Select an area within an image or select an object

 Select the Paint Bucket tool from the Toolbox

3 Click here in the Toolbox to access the Color Picker for changing the currently selected color

4 Click once on the selected area or object to change its color to the one loaded in the Paint Bucket tool

Gradient Tool

The Gradient tool can be used to add a gradient fill to a selection or an object. To do this:

1 Select an area in an image or select an object

2 Select the Gradient tool from the Toolbox

3 Click here in the Options bar to select preset gradient fills

4 Click on a gradient style to apply it as the default

145

Beware

If no selection is made for a gradient fill, the effect will be applied to the entire selected layer.

Hot tip

The default gradient effect in the Options bar is created with the currently selected foreground and background colors within the Toolbox.

...cont'd

5 Click here in the Options bar to access the Gradient Editor dialog box

Hot tip

To create a new preset gradient, create it in the Gradient Editor dialog box and click on the New button to add it to the list of preset gradients. Double-click on the gradient's icon to give it a unique name in the Gradient Name dialog box.

6 Click and drag the sliders to change the amount of a particular color in the gradient

7 Click along here to add a new color marker. Click on the OK button

8 Click an icon in the Options bar to select a gradient style

9 Click and drag within the original selection to specify the start and end points of the gradient effect

Don't forget

The amount that the cursor is dragged, when adding a gradient, determines where the centerpoint of the gradient is located and also the size of each segment of the gradient.

Brush and Pencil Tools

The Brush and Pencil tools work in a similar way and can be used to create lines of varying thickness and style. To do this:

1 Select the Brush tool or the Pencil tool from the Toolbox

2 Select the required options from the Options bar

3 Click and drag to create lines on an image. (The lines are placed directly on the image. To add lines without altering the background image, add a new layer above the background and add the lines on this layer. They will then be visible over the background.)

Impressionist Brush Tool

The Impressionist Brush tool can be used to create a dappled effect over an image, similar to that of an impressionist painting. To do this:

1 Select the Impressionist Brush tool from the Toolbox

2 Select the required options from the Options bar

3 Click and drag over an image to create an impressionist effect

Working with Color

All of the text and drawing tools make extensive use of color. Elements provides a number of methods for selecting colors, and also for working with them.

Foreground and background colors

At the bottom of the Toolbox there are two colored squares. These represent the currently selected foreground and background colors. The foreground color, which is the most frequently used, is the one that is applied to drawing objects, such as fills and lines, and also text. The background color is used for items, such as gradient fills, and for areas that have been removed with the Eraser tool.

Foreground color   Swap foreground and background colors

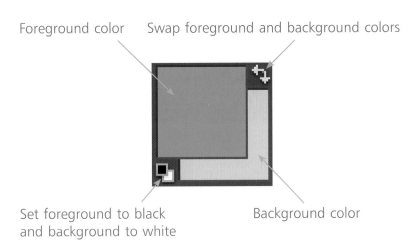

Set foreground to black and background to white   Background color

Hot tip

Whenever the foreground or background color squares are clicked on, the Eyedropper tool is automatically activated. This can be used to select a color from anywhere on your screen, instead of using the Color Picker.

Color Picker

The Color Picker can be used to select a new color for the foreground or background color. To do this:

1 Click once on the foreground or the background color square, as required

...cont'd

2 In the Color Picker, click to select a color

150

3 Click on the OK button

Color Swatches panel

The Color Swatches panel can be used to access different color panels that can then be used to select the foreground and background colors. To do this:

1 Select Window>Color Swatches from the Menu bar

2 Click here to access the available panels

9 Content and Effects

Adding special effects is one of the fun things about digital images. This chapter shows how to add a variety of these special effects.

About Content and Effects

Applying special effects can be one of the most satisfying parts of digital image editing: it is quick and the results can be dramatic. Elements has a range of Content and Effects that can be applied to images. To use these:

1 In the Editor, select Window>Content or Effects from the Menu bar to access the Content and Effects panels

The Content and Effects panels can only be accessed from the Editor, not the Organizer.

2 Within the Content panel click here to select a category for a particular topic

3 Click here to see all of the options for a particular category

Applying Effects

To apply special effects to an open image in the Editor:

1 Select the required item in the Effects panel

2 Click on the Apply button

Apply

3 Some effects, such as Filters, have additional dialog boxes in which a variety of settings can be specified in relation to how the effect operates and appears

Artwork

The Content panel can be used to add graphical elements to images. This can be done either to existing images or to a blank file, onto which other content can be added. To do this:

1 In the Editor, select File>New>Blank File from the Menu bar

2 Click here in the Content panel

3 Click on Backgrounds and select a background from the sub-category list

4 Click on the Apply button

5 The background is added to the blank file

6 Repeat step 3, but select a Frame option. This will then enable you to add an image, by clicking here or dragging an open image from the Project Bin

7 Repeat Step 3, but select the Graphics option to add a graphical element

8 Repeat Step 3, but select the Shapes option to add a 2D shape

Hot tip

If you save the final image as a Photoshop file (.PSD .PDD) you will still be able to open the image and edit each of the individual elements. However, if you save it as a JPEG, you will not be able to edit any of the artwork elements.

9 Save the final image in the same way as any other file

Themes

The Themes section of the Content panel can be used to add entire graphical themes to images. To do this:

 Open an image in the Editor and access the Content panel (Window>Content from the Menu bar)

 Click here and select a Themes category

Select an item within a specific category

Beware

If Themes are added to an image, its file size will increase considerably and the image processing speed will be slower when working with it on a computer.

Click on the Apply button

5 The Theme is applied to the open image

6 The elements of the Theme are displayed in the Layers panel

Don't forget

Themes are created by enabling the image element to show through a section of the background. This is displayed in the layers of the Layers panel.

7 Save the final image in the same way as any other file

Special Effects

Special Effects can be added to images from within the Effects panel. This can be accessed by selecting Window>Effects from the Menu bar. To add effects to images:

1 Open an image in the Editor

2 Click here to select the effects filter that can then be applied to the open image

3 Click next to Show All, to select a type of effect

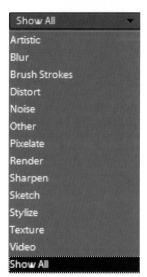

4 Or, click on one of the effects icons within the panel

5 Select the attributes for the selected effect and click on the OK button to apply it to the image

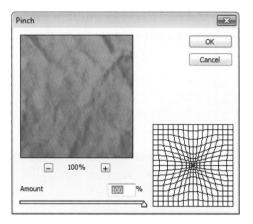

6 Layer Styles can be used to apply special effects to layers that have been added to an image

Don't forget

Layer Styles and Photo Effects are accessed by clicking on the button along the top of the Effects panel.

7 Photo Effects can be used to add artistic frames, or text panels, to an image

Text Effects

Text effects can be applied from the Content panel, to give text a more artistic appearance. To do this:

1 Open an image and select the Text option here in the Content panel

2 The available effects are displayed in the Text window

Don't forget

The font and size for Text Effects are the ones that were last used when normal text was applied. These appear in the text Options bar.

3 Select one of the Text Effects by double-clicking on it

4 Click on the Apply button

5 A text box, with text, is inserted in the image, with the selected Text Effect applied

6 To edit the text, select the Text tool from the toolbox

7 Select the text and enter the new text

8 To apply a different Text Effect, select the text box with the Move tool

9 Click on the text box

10 Select a new Text Effect in the Content panel

161

11 Click on the Apply button

Apply

12 The new Text Effect is applied to the selected text

Filtering Content

Due to the large amount of items in the Content panel, it is useful to be able to filter this according to the type of content that is required. To do this:

1 Click here in the Content panel

2 Select a category for displaying the types of content

3 Click on these buttons to filter the category of content according to (from left to right) Backgrounds, Frames, Graphics, Shapes, Text Effects and Themes

10 Sharing and Creating

Elements has a number of ways to share images, both with online services and with email. It also has numerous options for creating artistic effects, such as designed photo books and creative slide shows.

Saving Images for the Web

One of the issues for images that are going to be shared online is file size. This must be small enough so that the images can be downloaded quickly on a web page, or as an attachment in an email. To assist in this, Elements has a function for saving images in different formats and also altering the quality settings for each format. This enables you to balance the quality and file size, so that you have the optimum image for use online. To do this:

Don't forget

Preparing images for the Web is also known as optimizing them.

1 Open an image in the Editor and select File>Save for Web from the Menu bar

2 The original image is shown on the left of the Save for Web window

3 Select options for optimizing the image here

4 The preview of the optimized image is shown here, once the settings have been applied

5 The new file size and download time at a specified speed are shown below the image in the right hand panel

JPEG
116.7K
42 sec @ 28.8 Kbps

In Elements, the compression setting and the quality setting are linked, so that when one is altered the other is changed automatically.

6 Click here to select a file type and level of compression

OK

Cancel

Help

Preset: Custom

JPEG

Medium   Quality: 40

Progressive

ICC Profile   Matte:

7 Click here to select a quality setting

8 Enter new dimensions here to change the physical size of the image

Image Size
Original Size
Width: 798 pixels
Height: 1200 pixels

New Size
Width: 798 pixels
Height: 1200 pixels
Percent: 100
☑ Constrain Proportions
Apply

Even low-quality images can look good on web pages, as computer monitors are more forgiving in their image output than hard copy printing is.

9 Click on the OK button

OK

10 In the Save Optimized As window, save the image with a new name so that the original remains intact

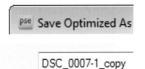

pse Save Optimized As

File name: DSC_0007-1_copy

About Share Mode

Share mode enables you to output your images in a variety of ways, and also send them to friends and family in different formats. Some of these involve third party services and these will vary depending on your own location. Also, some of the options offered through the Share mode require the video editing program, Elements Premiere. The standard options within Share mode are:

Don't forget

In the Mac version of Elements, the Share options are Web Photo Gallery, E-mail Attachments, CD/DVD and PDF Slide Show.

- **Online Album.** This can be used to display your photos online, using the available third party suppliers

- **E-mail Attachments.** This can be used to attach photos to emails via your email program

- **Photo Mail.** This can be used to produce creative email messages with your photos

- **Burn Video DVD/BluRay.** This requires Elements Premiere

- **Burn data CD/DVD.** This can be used to copy your photos to either CD or DVD

- **Online Video Sharing.** This requires Elements Premiere

- **Mobile Phones and Players.** This requires Elements Premiere

- **PDF Slide Show.** This can be used to create a slide show of your photos using the PDF format

Depending on your geographic location, there are additional Share options that can be accessed from the More Options link:

More Options ▶▶

PDF Slide Show...

Share with Kodak Easyshare Gallery ...

Share Video with Adobe Photoshop Showcase...

Send to SmugMug Gallery...

Send to CEIVA Digital Photo Frame ...

Share to Flickr...

Online Albums

One way of sharing images is to share them online. This can be done through the Online Album feature. To do this:

1 In either the Editor or the Organizer, click on the Share button and click on the Online Album button

2 Check on the Create New Album button and select how you would like to share the album

3 Click on the Next button

4 Images that were originally selected will be available in the album. Additional images can be dragged and dropped into the Content section. Give the album a name

5 Click on the Sharing tab and select a template for the album

6 Click on the Done button. You will be taken to a page, where you can register for the Photoshop Showcase service, to display and share your online album

Don't forget

Online Albums are created with Flash technology which produces very slick, professional animated designs for viewing images. However, this is all done in the background and you do not have to worry about the mechanics of how it is achieved.

Don't forget

Photoshop Showcase is an online photo sharing community where you can upload your own albums, and also view those of other users.

Creatively Emailing Images

One of the most common ways of transferring images electronically is by email. However, in addition to including images as simple attachments, it is also possible to produce creative emails where the image appears in a more artistic environment. This is done with a variety of artistic stationery and templates. To create artistic emails:

1 Open an image in the Editor, or select one in the Organizer

2 In either the Editor or the Organizer, click on the Share Button

3 Click on the Photo Mail button

4 The open image is inserted into the Photo Mail wizard

5 Click on the Next button

6 Enter a message to accompany the Photo Email

7 Click here to select a layout for the Photo Mail

8 Click on the Next Step button

9 Select options for customizing the layout of the Photo Mail

10 The image is attached to the email

About Create Mode

Image editing programs have now evolved to a point where there is almost as much emphasis on using images creatively as there is on editing them. Elements has an excellent range of options for displaying your images in some stunningly creative ways, called, appropriately enough, Create mode. These can be saved in the Organizer for viewing or sharing. To use Create mode:

Don't forget

In the Mac version of Elements, the Create options are Photo Book, Greeting Card, Photo Prints, Photo Collage, Web Photo Gallery and PDF Slide Show. These files are saved without the project icon shown in Step Four.

1 In either the Editor or the Organizer, click on the Create button

2 Select one of the Create options

Hot tip

To only view projects in the Organizer, select Find>By Media Type> Projects from the Organizer Menu bar.

3 Once a project has been saved it is displayed in the Organizer. This means that it can then be opened again and edited if required

4 A project file is denoted by this icon in the top right corner. Different projects have different icons

5 For a lot of the Create options there are themes and layout options that can be applied to the creations

171

6 To view more Create mode options, click on the More Options button at the bottom of the standard options

Photo Books

Several of the Create options follow a similar process. These
include Photo Books, Greeting Cards and Photo Collages. The
following process is for Photo Books, but it can similarly be
applied to the other two items.

1   Click on the Create button

2   Click on the Photo Book button

3   Select a layout
option for the
Photo Book

Photo Book

Layout Options

○ Random Photo Layout

● Choose Photo Layout

Page Size

A4 (210 mm x 297 mm) ▼

Choose a Theme

4   Select a Theme
for the Photo
Book layout

Additional Options

☑ Auto-Fill with Project Bin Photos

☐ Include Captions

Number of Pages   2

5   Click on the Create button   Create

6 Click in the middle of the creation to add images to the Photo Book, or drag any photos that are already open and available in the Project Bin here

7 Arrange images as required in the Photo Book

Don't forget

Once a Photo Book has been created, it can be saved as an individual file. This can be a large file, depending on the number of images in the Photo Book.

8 Use this toolbar to move through the Photo Book

Slide Shows

As traditional photographic slide shows are becoming more and more things of the past, electronic ones are taking their place with increasing frequency. This is an excellent way to display numerous images in artistic and appealing ways. In Elements, slide shows can be produced as a projects and then exported into a format that can be widely viewed. To create a slide show:

1 Open one, or more, images in the Editor or select them in the Organizer

2 In either the Editor or the Organizer, click on the Create button

3 Click on the Slide Show button

4 Select options for how you want the Slide Show to operate, such as slide duration, type of transition between slides and background music. Click on the OK button

5 The main Slide Show window is displayed

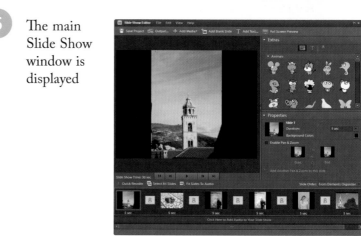

Don't forget

If an image is already selected in the Media Browser it will be the first one that is visible in the Slide Show window.

6 Use these buttons to preview the whole Slide Show

7 The images and transitions are displayed in the timeline. Click on a transition box to select a different one

8 Use these buttons to add graphics, text and narration to the Slide Show

9 Set the duration for each slide, and also whether panning and tilting is enabled, for when the Slide Show is viewed

Don't forget

Video and audio can be selected, either from the default collection in the Organizer or from your own collection elsewhere on your hard drive.

175

10 Click on the Add Media button to add more content to the Slide Show

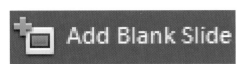

11 Click on the Add Blank Slide button if you want to include a blank slide.

This can then have content added to it in the same way as text and graphics and be used in a variety of ways, such as a title page for the Slide Show

...cont'd

12 Click on the Save Project button to save the file as a project. This can then be opened from the Organizer and edited

13 Click on the Output button, so that the Slide Show can be saved in a format that can be shared

14 The Slide Show Output window has options for saving the Slide Show

15 Select the use to which you want to put the Slide Show

16 Select the file type for how you want to save the Slide Show

17 Select any settings for the selected file type

18 Click on the OK button to save the Slide Show in the selected file format. This can be used to display the Slide Show and also share it with other people

VCDs

If you want to view your Slide Shows on television via a DVD player, or share them with other people in this format, this can be done by creating (writing) a VCD. This is similar to a DVD, except that it is created on a CD. This enables it to be played back on a DVD player, without the need to burn it onto a DVD disc with a DVD writer. To create a VCD:

1 Select a Slide Show project in the Organizer

2 Click on the Create button

3 Select More Options and click on the VCD with Menu button

4 The Slide Show selected in Step 1 is displayed in the Create a VCD with Menu window

5 If you want to include another Slide Show, click on the Add Slide Shows button and select another from the Organizer

6 Select the VCD format for the completed disc

Video Options

○ **NTSC**
   NTSC is used primarily in North America, Central America, and Japan.

○ **PAL**
   PAL is used primarily in European countries.

7 Click on the Burn button to create the VCD

Flipbooks

Flipbooks are dynamic projects that produce animated effects, in the same way as drawing similar pictures on pages in books and then flicking through them to create animated effects. To create a Flipbook:

1 Select similar images in the Organizer, or open them in the Editor

2 In either the Editor or the Organizer, click on the Create button

3 Select More Options and click on the Flipbook button

4 The Flipbook window has options for formatting the Flipbook

5 Select the speed, in frames per second, of the Flipbook and also select the output settings

6 Click on the Output button

7 The Flipbook will be saved as a Windows Media File (wmv). Select a location in which to save it and click on the Save button

(11) Printing Images

Calibrating Your Monitor

One of the issues with digital images is achieving consistency between different computer monitors and also output devices, such as printers. Inconsistency means that the colors can appear different if they are viewed on several monitors, and also that the colors in the printed image may not match those viewed on screen. One way to try to achieve as much consistency as possible is to calibrate your monitor before you start working with digital images. This is particularly important if you are going to be sharing images with other people for editing purposes, in which case they should calibrate their monitors too. This will ensure that images look as similar as possible on different machines, and so editing can be applied consistently.

To calibrate your monitor:

Don't forget

To access the Display properties, click the Start button and select Control Panel>Appearance and Personalization and select the Display button, then select the Change Display Settings option.

1 Make sure your monitor and computer have been turned on for at least 30 minutes

2 In the Control Panel, access the Display properties and set the monitor display to its highest resolution

3 In the Control Panel, access the Adobe Gamma option

 Adobe Gamma

Don't forget

If the Gamma option is not visible in the Control Panel, enter 'Gamma' into the Control Panel search box.

4 Check on the Step by Step (Wizard) box and click on the Next button to follow the wizard's steps

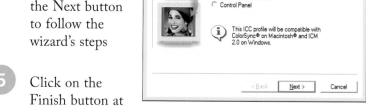

5 Click on the Finish button at the end of the wizard

6 Save the color profile that has been created

Print Size

Before you start printing images in Elements, it is important to ensure that they are going to be produced at the required size. Since the pixels within an image are not a set size, the printed dimensions of an image can be altered according to your needs. This is done by specifying how many pixels are used within each inch of the image. The more pixels per inch (ppi) then the higher the quality of the printed image, but the smaller in size it will be.

To set the print size of an image:

1 Open an image and select Image>Resize>Image Size from the Menu bar

2 Uncheck the Resample Image box. This will ensure that the physical image size, i.e. the number of pixels in the image, remains unchanged when the resolution is changed

3 The current resolution and document size (print size) are displayed here

4 Enter a new figure in the Resolution box (here the resolution has been increased from 200 to 300). This affects the Document size, i.e. the size at which the image prints

Print Options

The Print function can be used to view how an image will look when it is printed. To do this:

1 Open an image in the Editor, or select an image in the Organizer, and select File>Print from the Menu bar. The Print window has options for selecting a printer and its settings and size of paper

2 Click on these buttons to Add or Remove images to be printed

3 Click on the Select Print Size box to select the size at which you want the image to be printed. If you select Actual Size this will be produced according to the size set in the Image Size window, as shown on the previous page

Print Layouts

Rather than just offering the sole function of printing a single image on a sheet of paper, Elements has two options that can be used when printing images, which can help reduce the number of sheets of paper used.

Contact Sheets

This can be used to create and print thumbnail versions of a large number of images. To do this:

1. Access the Organizer and select the required images

2. Select File> Print from the Menu bar

3. Click under Select Type of Print and select Contact Sheet

4 Select Type of Print:

Contact Sheet

4. Click on the Print button. The selected images will be printed as thumbnails

Don't forget

When a contact sheet is created, new thumbnail images are generated. The original images are unaffected.

Don't forget

In the Mac version of Elements, the Contact Sheets and Picture Package options are available directly from the File menu in the main Editor window.

...cont'd

Picture Package

This can be used to print out copies of different images on a single piece of paper. To do this:

1 Access the Organizer and select the required images

2 Select File>Print from the Menu bar

3 Under Select Type of Print select the Picture Package print option

4 Select a Layout option and a Frame option

4 Select Type of Print:
Picture Package

5 Select a Layout:
A4 (10) 55x91

Select a Frame:
Antique Oval

5 The images are displayed as they will be when they are printed

Online Prints

Online printing of digital images is now firmly established and it is an excellent way of getting high quality, economical, prints without leaving the comfort of your own home.

1 Open an image, or images, in either the Editor, or select them in the Organizer. Click on the Create button

2 Click on the Photo Prints button

3 There are options for printing images on your own printer, and also services for online prints. These will be specific to your own location. When you click on one of the services you will be taken to their website, from where you will be able to order your online prints. Most services will also have an option for uploading your photos, so that they can be viewed online

Hot tip

When printing images, either online or on your own printer, make sure that they have been captured at the highest resolution setting on your camera, to ensure the best printed quality.

185

Creating PDF Files

PDF (Portable Document Format) is a file format that is used to maintain the original formatting and style of a document, so that it can be viewed on a variety of different devices and types of computers. In general, it is usually used for documents that contain text and images, such as information pamphlets, magazine features and chapters from books. However, image files, such as JPEGs, can also be converted into PDF and this can be done within Elements without the need for any other special software. To do this:

Don't forget

PDF files are an excellent way to share files so that other people can print them. All that is required is a copy of Adobe Acrobat Reader, which is bundled with most software packages on computers, or can be downloaded from the Adobe website at:
www.adobe.com

1 Open a file and select File>Save As from the Menu bar

2 Select a destination folder and make sure the format is set to Photoshop PDF. Then click Save

3 The PDF file is created and can be opened in Adobe Acrobat or Elements

Index

U

V

W

Z